Heaven
and the
Angels

H. A. Baker

Trumpet Press, Lawton, OK

HEAVEN and the ANGELS

BY
H. A. BAKER
Miaoli, Formosa

Missionary to Tibet, China, and Formosa Author of, The Three Worlds, Visions Beyond the Veil, Plains of Glory and Gloom, and other books.

[H. A. Baker published all his books with the above notice of no copyright. This edition has corrected spelling and edited photos, with Scripture references in the text rather than the appendix.]

ISBN: 9781477556290

Library of Congress Catalog-in-Publication Data

Author: Baker, H. A.
Title: Heaven and The Angels
1. Visions 2. Heaven 3. Angels 4. Life after death

Trumpet Press

CONTENTS

CHAPTERS

Publisher's Preface

Harold Armstrong Baker (1881–1971) was an American author and Pentecostal missionary to Tibet from 1911 to 1919; then to China from 1919 to 1950 when he and his wife, Josephine, were forced to leave the mainland for Taiwan, from 1955 until his death in 1971.

The Bakers started *Adullam Rescue Mission* for street children in Yunnan Province, China. The children in the home, mostly boys aged from six to eighteen, had a revival during which they had visions of heaven, Paradise, angels, and even hell. These visions were recounted in Baker's book *Visions Beyond the Veil*.

This book, *Heaven and the Angels*, includes information from the orphan boys' visions, but also includes accounts from many people from around the world during the past two centuries who had dreams, visions, and angelic visits right here on Earth.

The book was originally published about 1940, and some of the original pictures were of such poor quality that they could not be reproduced, but most of them are included here.

TO THE READER

Although for many years I have been a missionary in China for the express purpose of guiding man out of darkness into the land of endless light, at the same time, I must confess, I had most vague ideas of that land toward which we journeyed. I believed heaven was a land of eternal bliss where we worshipped God in His presence. The saints in heaven were, in my opinion, airy angel-like beings who were inexpressibly happy. There was, of course, the New Jerusalem with golden streets and the Throne of God. Beyond these conceptions of heaven all else was vague, misty and unreal in my mind.

The baptism of the Holy Spirit had made Jesus and life in Him very real, and heaven and eternal life had also become living realities. But I had few definite ideas of heaven. Then there came a mighty outpouring of the Holy Spirit upon the orphanage of Chinese children that we conducted for ten years. At that time these children who had even more vague ideas of heaven than I had were, day after day and night after night, caught away in the spirit to see the realms of the eternal worlds. The curtain that separates the temporal from the eternal was drawn aside and the children saw wonders of heaven and the life beyond the grave. The account of these experiences is written in my book, *VISIONS BEYOND THE VEIL*, now in its fourth edition, and translated into three languages.

My eyes were opened to the wonders of the life beyond the grave. The importance of a better knowledge of these realities having come to me strongly, it seemed to be the work of the Lord to bring to my hand tracts, letters and books from different corners of the earth, dealing with visions beyond the veil, such as had come so unexpectedly to our orphan children. it was marvelous to read how the experiences of others checked in detail with those given the Chinese children. Nowhere was there disagreement.

I was amazed, too, to find that most wonderful and detailed visions of the life to come had been given to saints of God from time to time and that some inspiring books and tracts have been circulated in various lands in, or before, the last century. The reading of these revelations, as well as the visions given our orphan children, under the anointing of the Holy Spirit, have made to me the life beyond the grave a land of realities, while the things of this earth have become more and more the misty shadows.

Because I had been in such ignorance of the life of the world to come, and because these revelations have so transformed my own life and my work on the mission field, I felt led to gather together the best of the things that had come to my knowledge in one way and another, and to put the material in book form available to my friends at home. The Lord has greatly blessed with gifts of the Holy Spirit many of the people of the ten tribes with whom I work in the mountains of Yunnan, West China. Many who formerly had no conception of a Paradise and the City of God have been caught up in the spirit to see the very things related in this book.

In view of these experiences I firmly believe that, although the reader may find many things herein related new to him, as they were to me, nevertheless, they will be found to be true revelations from God of the life beyond the grave.

Will the reader first of all please read the "Cloud of Witnesses" and note the books quoted, and the tracts, and publications from well-known publishers, whose publications in their time were considered orthodox by the churches of their day. It will be seen, too, that many of the writers from whom I quote were men whose sane views of the things of God and whose spiritual life were not questioned.

Since this book is in some ways unique and deals with questions of great importance, will the reader carefully and open-mindedly read the *Introduction* in Chapter 1? I hope that this will prepare all readers to accept, as I do, the truth of these revelations as messages of God to men.

I found it impracticable and unnecessary to quote authority in detail for all the statements herein given. In some instances I have given direct quotations and in others I cited the authority of persons whose visions substantiate certain statements. In many places I make definite statements with further substantiation. I want to make clear that in what I have not given as direct quotations, or without reference to authority, there are no statements so far as I am aware, made in this book that are not backed by direct revelations in visions, or by the principles arising therefrom, or coming from other special revelations from the Lord. Where definite statements are made that seem rather startling and dogmatic, let it be borne in mind that these are not unwarranted assertions, but truths revealed in the body of the material that is the source of authority for this volume.

Since the land to which we journey should be of greatest concern and interest in this present life, we should find out all we can about that blessed land of Promise. Accordingly, will the readers of this book who have further revelations concerning the subjects herein discussed, or who have, or know, of other books and tracts dealing with these revelations, or who know of persons raised from the dead, be kind enough to send such information to our home representative, . . . (This information is 60-70 years old.)

Please help in spreading these truths by loaning your book to friends. A book can travel far. Help them go. Keep yours moving.

[The scripture references have been put into the book so you don't have to look them up, therefore, that section has been removed.]

H. A. Baker.

THE CLOUD OF WITNESSES
(Bibliography)

I. The Witness of Visions

I. Books:

Signs and Wonders, by Mrs. M. B. Woodworth-Etter, contains an account of a vision given O. G. Wood, an infidel co-worker with Robert Ingersoll, who, still in a state of infidelity and rebellion against God, was caught up to heaven while he lay in a state of trance for twenty-four hours. This and other cases show that visions are not given on the basis of especial spiritual experiences, or a close walk with God. This infidel was later converted at the age of eighty-two and healed of a crippled condition that had lasted for fifteen years. (Book out of print).

Acts of the Holy Ghost, by M. B. Woodworth-Ether, page 321. (Out of print).

From the Jaws of Death, Conference Press, 912 Belmont Avenue, Chicago, Illinois.

Intra Muros, by Rebecca Ruther Springer. David C. Cook Publishing Co., Elgin, Illinois.

Visions of the Spiritual World, by Sadhu Sundar Singh. An account of the remarkable visions of this well-known Hindu saint who lived so selflessly, worldlessly, and Christ-like on earth and who was repeatedly caught up to heaven in vision. The MacMillin Co., Madras, India.

The Sadhu, by Streeter and Appasamy. The MacMillin Co, Madras, India.

Visions of Heaven and Hell, by John Bunyan. The Gospel Publishing House, Springfield, Missouri.

Visions Beyond the Veil, by H. A. Baker, Christ Mission, Youngstown, Ohio.

Miracles of Today, by J. W. Adams, M. A.; foreword by Stephen Jeffreys. Out of print. Mr. Adams, a vicar of the Church of England, associated with Stephen Jeffreys in some of his wonderful campaigns in England. From childhood Mr. Adams was one of those persons, by no means uncommon, who could see through the veil that hides the world of spirits. In Chapter 6, of Sixty Years With Spirits, he corroborates what is in this present volume in so far as he touches on the same points. (Book out of print).

Scenes Beyond the Grave, by Marietta Davis, who for nine days, free from any sickness, lay in a state of trance from which she could not be awakened. During that time in vision she was caught up to heaven to see conditions in the Infant Paradise. She also saw in part other sections of heaven as well as parts of hell. Her book was written one hundred years ago. (Out of print).

II. Tracts:

In Heaven, But Not of Heaven, an account of a vision given to General William Booth, founder of the Salvation Army. Free Tract Society, 746 Crocker Street, Los Angeles, California.

A Vision of a Wesleyan Lady, recorded by Robert Young, a missionary who lived in the same station as the woman who had seen this remarkable vision. She seemed to visit the other world the seven days in which she lay in a trance with no sign of life in her body, except a slight foaming at the mouth and a little warmth in the region about her heart. It was impossible to arouse her out of this state. Free Tract Society, 746 Crocker Street, Los Angeles, California.

A Vision of Heaven and Hell, given to Pauline Cox, 258 Beaver Street, Akron, Ohio. This woman lay in a trance for sixty hours, after which time the doctors, after making many examinations without finding the cause of her condition, gave up the case. Gospel Publishing House, Springfield, Mo.

A Visit to Paradise, printed by Walter J. Mortlock, "Beulah" Hilltop Road, Ferndown, Darst, England

A Vision of Heaven and Hell, by E. Cooper. Emanuel Bible Tract Dopot, Box 6114, Ballard Station, Seattle, Washington.

A Remarkable Vision of Heaven and Hell, by Flora Reid Coate, Faith Publishing House, 920 W. Manslu Avenue, Guthrie, Oklahoma.

III. Periodicals:

Talmage's Vision of Heaven, published October, 1936, in *Word*

and Work, Christian Workers Publishing Co., Farmingham, Mass.

My Vision, Charles S. Price, published in *Golden Grain*, January, 1940, 2100 Bridgen Road, Pasadena, California.

His Guardian Angel, article in *Redemption Tidings*, Nov. 20, 1936.

IV. Personal Letters:

Letter from Rev. Reinberg, Gladwin, Michigan.

Letter from Harman S. Matz, Colorado Springs, Colorado.

Letter from Charles A. Davis, 352 Carlton Avenue, Brooklyn, New York.

Letter from Mae Villa, 143 South Alma Avenue, Los Angeles , California.

Letter from Nevada Trimble, Phillipi, West Virginia.

V. Personal Contacts:

In addition to all the written accounts of visions and revelations referred to in this bibliography, another very considerable amount of unwritten evidence in exact harmony has come to me in my personal contacts in missionary work among the mountain tribes in south-west China.

Many of these visions and revelations were given to people who had no previous knowledge or understanding of what they saw in vision; nevertheless, the things seen and the revelations received were in complete harmony with the Bible and with what is found in the sources mentioned in this bibliography and in other parts of this volume.

II. Witness of Persons Raised From the Dead
I. Books:

With Signs Following, by S. H. Frodsham, page 155. This book contains the record of Mrs. Vex, who knew distinctly that she was dying, even when she took her last breath. She was dead two and one-half hours. Gospel Publishing House, Springfield, Missouri.

The Three Worlds, by H. A. Baker, p. 284-294 and other instances.

12 Kargar Fulla (12 sermons preached in Sweden, 1929), translated. Account of Mrs. Booth-Clibborn being raised from the dead after four hours.

II. Tracts:

Made Alive From the Dead by the Power of God, by Mrs. Maude J. Keer, who died and rose again. Free Tract Society. 745 Crocker Street, Los Angeles , California.

III. Periodicals:

Raised From the Dead, an account of the case of Miss Laura Johnson as given in *Word and Work*, December, 1937; *The Comforter*, February. 1938. *The Daily Clarion Ledger*, Jackson, Miss., and in various papers of the Associated Press throughout the United States. This girl, spoken of by the Press as "The Miracle Girl", while near death in terrible agony from a combination of awful afflictions, went into a trance during which time she was caught up to heaven. Shortly after this experience she died. Although she died with hopeless, incurable afflictions of many years, when raised from the dead she was every whit healed. For eleven days she could walk only on the tips of her toes, praising the Lord with uplifted hands.

Laura Johnson, the "miracle girl", who was raised from the dead, reported throughout the country by the Associate press, and used by the Lord to heal the sick and lead multitudes to Christ.

During this time she neither ate nor slept. In this condition she was visited by representatives of the Press, and the miracle was reported in secular papers throughout the country. During the time mentioned thousands of people came to see the "Miracle Girl." Great numbers of those who came were healed of their diseases and afflictions when prayed for by Miss Johnson.

A Modern Miracle, by W. W. Simpson, and published in the Pentecostal Evangel. This is the account of a Chinese who died in Shanghai. After being prepared for burial he came to life, relating that he had seen the world beyond.

Many of his own family and friends, none of whom had been favorable to Christianity, were converted. *Pentecostal Evangel*, Gospel Publishing House, Springfield, Missouri. The Latter Rain Fellowship, December, 1935.

A Dead Man Comes Back to Life, by Harry A. Miller of the Africa Inland Mission. *Moody Monthly*, April 4. 1937.

"We believe what you tell us about heaven, and the Lord has made it so real in our hearts by the Holy Spirit that we know we have the down- payment, the "earnest." But some of my Chinese friends want to know if anybody has ever been to heaven and seen it."

"Yes, I have a friend who died and went to heaven and returned. The wife of another friend of mine also died and went to heaven and came back. I have letters about many such."

IV. Personal Letters:

"Three Persons Raised From the Dead." These cases occurred in Chili, South America, and the accounts, written in the *Chile Pentecostal*, November, 1937, and March, 1919, are translated into English and verified by Missionary W. C. Hooper in a letter now in the hands of the present writer.

"*A Child of Five Years Raised From the Dead.*" This account appeared in the *Pentecostal Evangel*. In order to get more details I wrote to the pastor of this girl. Her pastor, M. Gensichen, Friedrichscrurer Strasso 25, Germany, under date of August 30, 1938, wrote me in careful detail the circumstances of the death and restoration to life of this child.

The child died of diphtheria and was carried to heaven by an angel. When raised from the dead she was entirely well, and arising she insisted that she must have something to eat and have her doll to play with. Heaven had seemed so wonderful, and the earth so dirty that, after her experience, she did not want to live on earth. Although she had a loving Christian mother, at Christmas time when the mother asked her what nice thing she wanted for Christmas a doll, a ball, some nice clothes, or what—the child said, "No, I want to die and go back to heaven."

CHAPTER 1
INTRODUCTION

I believe that the visions recorded in this book are reliable revelations from God and that when this present life is ended I shall, with rapture in the realms of the redeemed behold the very things herein described in part. I believe this for the following reasons:

I. Visions given by God, as recorded in the Bible, were considered as reliable as any facts of visible life.

This was true in the days of the Old Testament. The prophets in Old Testament days, having received revelations from God when they were in a state of trance, or were caught away in the spiritual realms of the Lord in vision, delivered to Israel the revelations and messages they then received as wholly reliable from God. Thus did Isaiah, Jeremiah, Daniel and all the other Old Testament prophets declare their message to Israel to be proclamations backed by divine authority. Israel was always held accountable to God for thus accepting, or rejecting, these messages coming through visions.

In the New Testament, also, visions were accepted and acted upon as having full authority and as being as reliable as any other way of revealing facts to, or between, men. For instance, an angel speaking to Joseph in a vision in a dream was considered full divine authority upon which he acted and fled into Egypt with Mary and Jesus. It was likewise in response to a vision that they returned from Egypt. Joseph considered the angel that he saw in a dream in vision as much a fact, or reality, as he did seeing men face to face. Visions given to Cornelius, Peter, Paul and others were likewise considered and acted upon as realities.

"I know a man in Christ—caught up to the Third Heaven—caught up to Paradise", Paul writes. "Whether in the body, or out of the body, I cannot tell", he further adds. But clearly there is a Paradise in the Third Heaven, and in vision it was real as life in earth.

Accordingly, we can believe that the visions recorded in the following chapters are views and revelations of realities because both the Old Testament and the New Testament assure us that visions are views of realities.

II. Visions were Continued Throughout the Church Age.
That visions as given in the Old and New Testament days were to
continue through the whole of the church age is clearly stated in the
scripture: "It shall come to pass in the last days, saith God, I will
pour out of my Spirit Upon all flesh—and your young men shall see
visions" (Acts 2:17 29. Ezek. 47). Therefore, visions are to be a part
of the churches' experience in our day, for the "last days" are not yet
finished.

Tribal young men and women Christians, Yunnan province, China,
who help fulfill this scripture: "It shall come to pass in the last days,
saith God, I will pour out of My Spirit upon all flesh; and your sons and
your daughters shall prophesy, and your young men shall see vision"
(Acts 2:17). "And on my servants and on my handmaidens I will pour
out in those days of my Spirit; and they shall prophesy" (Acts 2:18).

Some of these tribesmen do have visions. Some of these handmaidens do prophesy.

When on the Day of Pentecost Peter repeated the promise that in
the "last days" young men should see visions he, in no way, even
hinted that such days of visions were to end, or be affected by the
conclusion of the writing of the New Testament. At that time no
word of the New Testament had yet been written, nor is there any
place that even suggests that the recording of a part, probably a
small part, of the visions following the Day of Pentecost would, in
any way, curtail the continuance of God-given revelations through
visions just as this method of revelation had continued from the be-

ginning of His dealings with man. Whether visions be recorded in the Bible, or elsewhere, in no way affects their original divine authority.

Since visions were to continue throughout the Church age, we have reason to believe that visions as recorded in this present volume may carry as much divine authority and sanction as those recorded in the Bible, the only difference being in the degree of perfection with which the visions are set forth in writing.

III. The Lord's Revelations are Progressive. Because of this we can believe that such visions and revelations as recorded in this book are to be accepted at full value as progressive revelations of the Lord to His people. From Adam to Moses, from Moses to Christ, from Christ to Calvary, from Calvary to Pentecost, from Pentecost to Revelation—from the beginning of Genesis to the end of Revelation, God's revelations to His children, being progressive, are sufficient evidence that His children subsequent to Bible days will still receive revelations in addition to those received in Bible days.

Some of the Adullum Orphanage Chinese children upon whom the Holy Spirit was poured forth as in New Testament days, giving them visions of heaven and the unseen worlds as real as scenes in the present world. Like Paul, they were caught up to Paradise, whether in the body, or out of the body, like Paul, they could not tell. They thought they left their bodies and went to heaven. What they saw corresponded exactly with what was seen by those who died and actually went to heaven and came back.

We have the definite promise of further progressive revelations, in Jesus' own words that when the Holy Spirit should come after His ascension the Spirit would reveal to the saints things "to come" in the future. (John 16:13). It is, therefore, consistent with the Scripture that in present day revelations the children of the Lord should receive enlarged visions and additional progressive visions of the New Jerusalem and the New World and other things of the eternal world, following less complete revelations given to John and saints of old. Furthermore, these modern saints, like John of old, were told to "write", or otherwise make their progressive visions and revelations known to men on earth, especially to God's own children.

IV. Such Visions as Recorded in This Book Would Not Come from Satan. The very nature of these visions, making known the glories of heaven and the wonders of God's redeeming love is sufficient proof that they did not come from a satanic source. Satan would never give such revelations of the joys of heaven prepared for those who escape his power, nor would he reveal the horrors of hell and his own awful doom and that of his demons and his dupes among men.

In the second place we know definitely that these visions and revelations do not come from satanic sources because the Bible clearly teaches that evil spirits of false prophecy will not confess that Jesus is God come in the flesh, as do all the visions and prophesies and revelations recorded in this volume. (I John 4 :1, 2). In all the visions herein considered, it will be seen that Jesus is everywhere and in every way exalted. His cross, His resurrection from the dead, His exaltation above all powers on earth and in heaven, His redeeming grace among the children of men, and all that makes Him both God and man are things that shine out clearly in the glory-light that radiates from heaven in all of these visions and God-given revelations. Both the spirit and the teachings of these visions are divine not satanic.

V. These Visions and Revelations Were Not of Human Origin. In the first place, in many cases those who had seen these visions had no previous knowledge of such things as they saw, nor did they believe in the reality of such. This was true in the case of Bunyan, Sundar Singh, and of Marietta Davis, all of whose remarkable visions cover all the essential details given in other visions recorded. In fact, before these three persons had been given visions they even doubted the realities of heaven itself, to say nothing of such glories as the Lord revealed to them. Had they written before their visions from what knowledge they then possessed, they all would have written contrary to what they wrote subsequent to their visions. John Bunyan so doubted the reality of heaven that he was on his way to commit suicide when the Lord gave him his wonderful vision. Sundar Singh, likewise, driven by doubts, would have ended his life in a few hours had Jesus not appeared to him and given him visions. Marietta Davis was so uncertain of eternal realities that she refused to become a member of the Church of God.

In the second place, these visions could not have been the product of the subconscious mind. For instance, the Chinese woman in Shan Tung, China, had never heard of, or even dreamed of the New Jerusalem, or any of the glories which she saw when she died and which later she described in perfect accord with the Bible. Similar instances were given the Chinese children in The Adullam Orphanage, as well as many other authentic cases.

This beggar boy from the streets of Kunmimg, Yunnan, China, was as uneducated, incapable, unpromising, and as much of an off-scouring of the earth as he looks to be. He knew enough to believe the gospel and knew little more. He was an extreme contrast, naturally and spiritually, to the highly qualified, deeply spiritual, godly saint, Sundar Singh. Yet the Lord, time after time, gave this boy many of the same visions of heaven's greatest wonders that He gave the Sundar.

Visions are given as the Lord sees best by "grace" and not on the basis of intellectual or spiritual qualifications.

This dull boy never had any previous conception of such a Paradise as he was led by the Holy Spirit to see.

In the third place, such visions could not have been of human origin because they were beyond human conception. No literature, prose, or poem has ever set forth such an ideal, perfect and glorious Utopia as the sublimest hope of man in an ideal state as is revealed in these visions. Since they far exceed the loftiest flights of human imagination. they must have been of divine origin.

In the fourth place, the very language with which these visions are described shows their divine nature and the hand of God in their recording. And so it is apparent that these visions are not of human origin, for:

1. They could not have been the result of previous knowledge; or

2. have come from the subconscious mind; or

3. have been the product of human conception of an ideal hereafter; or

4. have been described in such beautiful language by the unaided natural talents of the writers.

VI. These visions claim to Be Revelations From God to Man. In many instances the persons receiving these visions say that they were told in heaven to write what they saw and tell these visions to men, much like John was told to write Revelations "in a book to be sent to all the churches." Whether or not the written account of these visions is as much inspired as the book of Revelations in no way detracts from the fact that these revelations claim to be revelations of heavenly realities intended to be made known to man on earth.

VII. Those Seeing Visions Believed They Saw Realities. All the persons who saw the visions recorded in this volume believed they saw true realities. To them the earth and all it contains appeared as temporal, fleeting shadows; whereas the realms of highest heaven, they were convinced, were the true, eternal realities.

When in heaven these visitors were frequently told that after their return to earth for a brief sojourn to complete their service for the Lord they would be exalted back to heaven forever to enjoy the very life and conditions they in wonder then beheld. This same assurance applied to those caught up to the celestial realms while still "in the body", as well as to those who, while their bodies were dead, went to heavenly realms "out of the body."

After these experiences, all alike believed that they saw real things, not shadows. Thereafter they all lived zealous Christian lives in preparation for the day they would enter what they were sure was the world of realities which they had already seen.

Believing in these heavenly realities Bunyan wrote his *Pilgrim's Progress*, which book is used in pointing men to the land of realities.

Sundar Singh, before whom thousands sat almost entranced as he told them of the land beyond the grave and the way thereto, preached under the power of the Holy Spirit largely that he received by visions and revelations. He doubted if he could have persevered in his life of hardships in Tibet had it not been for the strength and assurance received from his heavenly visits when in frequent trances.

Thus, too, did William Booth after seeing heaven in a vision become so certain that he had seen the real life, in part, and real things on heaven's shore that in his full assurance and faith he became the source of power to start the great work of the Salvation Army that still sweeps around the world.

We need not add, or multiply such testimonies, but sum them all up in one statement: those who had visions of the unseen spiritual world all believed that they had seen realities and that in heaven after death they would enjoy the very same things that they had seen before their death.

More than that, they were told in some instances that they were to return to earth and make known to men what they had seen and that it was for this purpose they had been permitted to visit the heavenly world. At no time was there any hint that the things they had seen were less than realities—heaven's plains, Paradises, New Jerusalem, and all heavenly life as set forth on the following pages.

VIII. The Fruits Resulting From These Visions Were Divine. The effect these visions had upon the persons who saw them shows that they were from the Lord. Bunyan, who was in such a state of depressing doubt and on the verge of self destruction when rescued by his vision, was transformed into a saint of God. And as we know, Sundar Singh was saved by his vision from suicide to become a saint so transformed that children, seeing him, mistook him for Jesus. Marietta Davis, a doubter, became by her vision a firm Christian of faith. William Booth, a weak Christian, because of his vision became a flaming fire of God. Time and space would fail us were we to write of all who have been rescued from infidelity and the powers of Satan through personal visions.

As surely as Paul, on the road to Damascus, was converted and became a new and different man because of a revelation from heaven, so surely were many others changed into new creatures through their own visions related on these pages.

Therefore, the results of these visions upon those who received them, turning them into great saints of God, show that He gave the visions. "A tree is known by its fruit." Visions bearing Godly fruit are from a Godly tree.

Moreover, the effect of these visions on other men show that they were from God. Sundar Singh, General Booth and John Bunyan converted through their visions, were used of the Lord in saving multitudes of lost men. The account of Marietta Davis' visions as she sent them forth encouraged the faith of saints around the world. Without advertising, her book rapidly went through twenty-three editions and it was eagerly and profitably read by Christians of all sects and denominations. These are but a few of many who, being converted through visions and then preaching what was thereby revealed, have led countless numbers—multitudes to final redemption through faith in Christ and His blood, while additional numbers of saints have been strengthened in their spiritual life.

SADHU SUNDAR SINGH

Having forsaken wealth and fame for Jesus' sake, he became the most popular Christian in India and well known throughout the Christian world. He was probably the most Christ-like saint of the last century. He spent much time in heaven in vision.

Accordingly, these visions are shown to be from God:

1. Because of their effect upon the persons receiving them, and

2. Their effect upon the world.

IX. The Perfect Checking of These Visions With the Bible Proves All to Be of the Same Origin as the Bible—all From God. The very principles and teachings in these visions and revelations in all respects check perfectly with the principles set forth in the Bible. The principles and teachings of Jesus rebuking all the things of the kingdom of Satan in hundreds of instances, without a single exception, by "the law of probabilities" prove that these visions and the Bible are from the same source, a common source alone accounting for such unbroken harmony.

Then again, the descriptions of Paradise and the New Jerusalem, in so far as they coincide with descriptions in the Bible, check exactly. Where visions cover more details and a wider range than given in the Bible, they all are still in consistent harmony with what is in the Bible, thus showing the common source of these visions and the visions in the Word of God.

X. Furthermore, the Perfect Agreement With one Another as With the Bible of so Many Visions in so Many Hundreds of Details Shows Them to be Divine. The visions recorded in this volume, as well as hundreds of similar visions not herein related, were given to persons of all stages of spiritual development in many different lands, to people of many different languages, and to persons who were separated by decades or centuries of times, and to people who had not communicated with one another. All this proves that these visions and revelations are supernatural. The mathematical "law of chances" shows that any other explanation is impossible. Were these visions not all from one God-given source, disagreement in many details, even countless details, would be inevitable—a mathematical demonstration.

Such checking in archeological findings in hundreds of details, without any findings that do not check with the Bible, is considered scientific proof that the Bible and these findings are alike true. Because of this, the world's first rank archeologists have come to accept the Bible as true. Likewise the agreement of these visions and the Bible in such hundreds of details without any contrary disagreement shows that the visions and the Bible are harmonious witnesses of realities—science proof.

XI. Persons, While in Vision, Seeing the Things in Heaven, Or in Hell, Saw Others who Died at that Exact Time Enter These Realms. Take, for instance, the authentic account of Miss D., the Wesleyan lady, which we shall quote. This missionary was thought to be dying at the end of a protracted illness. Although the attending friends thought her dead, since the symptoms of death did not set in they found that she had gone into a trance from which she did not awaken for nearly a week. Then "she opened her eyes and said: 'Mr. C. is dead.' " Her attendants, thinking she was delirious, replied that she was mistaken as Mr. C. was not only alive, but well.

"'Oh, no', said she. 'He is dead, for a short time ago, as I passed the gates of hell, I saw him descend into the pit and the blue flame covered him. Mr. B. is also dead, for he arrived in heaven just as I was leaving that happy place, and I saw the beautiful gates thrown wide open to receive him and I heard the host of heaven shout, 'Welcome, weary pilgrim.' "

Mr. C. was a neighbor and a very wicked person; Mr. B. who lived at no great distance, was A good old man, for many years a consistent and useful member of the Church of God. The parties who heard Miss D's startling and confident statement immediately sent to make inquiries about the two individuals alluded to, and found to their utter astonishment that the former had dropped dead about a half hour before, while in the act of tying his shoe, and at about the same time the latter had suddenly passed into the eternal world. For the truth of this I do solemnly vouch. This is quoted from the account of Robert Young, a young missionary in India, who visited this lady just prior to her trance and many times during the trance and immediately after she came out of the trance. I know of similar instances that cannot be given for lack of space. The fact that the men who died were seen thus entering realms seen in vision at that exact time is evidence that the other things simultaneously seen were also realities.

XII. In Visions of Paradise and the New Jerusalem Friends and Relatives Who Previously Died Were Frequently Seen in Spiritual, Glorified Bodies Among the Hosts of the Redeemed Saints in Heaven. That these persons seen and conversed with were in fact real persons is proven, among other instances, in the case of Sundar Singh.

One time, when in vision, he was talking with the saints in Paradise a man in a glorious heavenly body came up to him and asked if he remembered him. When the Sundar replied in the negative, this stranger explained that before his death he was a leper in a certain asylum that the Sundar had visited. "I then had a filthy, leprous body, not like the one in which you now find me", he said. He then told the Sundar the year, the month and the day he had died. The

Sundar investigated this and found that such a man had been in that particular asylum and had died on the exact day that, in Paradise, he had told the Sundar he had died.

Other similar instances are on record, but this one authentic case is sufficient to prove the point that the views of spiritual realms in vision are views of realities. The relatives and other saints seen in the various realms of heaven are but a part of these realms of mansions and trees and flowers and animal life and superlative park-like wonders of heaven's glory life. Since all these wonders in the realms of heaven are co-related, coordinated and interwoven into one united whole, is it not true that to prove the reality of any one part of this co-ordination is to prove other parts to be realities? Accordingly, to prove the reality of one saint in heaven, as in the case of the one seen by Sundar Singh, must be considered sufficient proof of the reality of other saints so often seen in heaven by great numbers of persons caught up into these realms in visions. At the same time it also indicates that whatever else they see are real objects.

She Djen Fu with two Adullam orphans, one blind and one deficient. She Djen Fu was the first Adullam boy to die and go to heaven. He was frequently seen there by other Adullam children when they were caught up to the third heaven in vision.

XIII. The Testimony of Persons Raised from the Dead Corroborates These Visions. I have the authentic account of almost a score of persons who were raised from the dead. So far as I have been able to secure the personal testimony of these persons as regards their experience while they were out of their dead bodies, all who reached the gates of the New Jerusalem or were permitted to enter therein saw in their real experience exactly what others saw in vision as realities.

Aside from the foregoing twelve proofs of the realities seen in vision, this one coming from the dead should alone be sufficient evidence to convince any unprejudiced mind, it seems to me. Is not the testimony of truthful eye witnesses considered satisfactory proof in all the courts of men? Criminals in all courts of the world are executed upon the testimony of eye-witnesses and upon only circumstantial evidence. I suppose much more than ninety per cent of our beliefs of history, science, geography and other studies is founded upon the testimony of eye-witnesses or upon circumstantial evidence. I have not seen personally one city out of a thousand; yet, I believe in the reality of these places because of the testimony of others who have been there. Although I have never been to New York, I believe there is a New York and I know something of its subways through the testimony of friends who have been there. Likewise, although I have not personally been to the New Jerusalem in the Third Heaven, I believe it is there and I know something of its streets and beauty because of the testimony of truthful friends whom I personally know and of others I know indirectly. What better proof of the realities of the visions seen in heaven could I ask than that of my friends and of others who have been there?

We should not wonder at this method used by the Lord to make the realities of our eternal home unmistakably known to us. A few were raised from the dead in Old Testament days. A few, not many, but a sufficient number, were raised from the dead in New Testament days to prove the power of Jesus over death. In recent years a sufficient number of persons have been raised from the dead to answer the Lord's purpose in making known to the present generation what needs to be made known about the world to come. All this we have a right to expect. Did Jesus not say that the works He did, His followers throughout the ages would be able to do? (John 14:12). And does this not include the raising of the dead?

That these persons in our day actually died, left their bodies; ascended to the New Jerusalem in the Third Heaven, and then returning to earth again, entered their bodies they had discarded, is shown by all the circumstantial evidence men universally consider satisfactory proof.

I cannot enter into all these circumstances in detail. I can now only point out that in the cases of some score of persons who came to my attention, they themselves believed they had died. Their friends who stood by their death beds, saw them die, saw them go, and saw them return. These witnesses, several score, believe those who died gave a true report of where they had gone and of what they saw while out of the body.

Surely so many persons who died and so many death bed witnesses could not all have been mistaken. "The law of chances" forbids this. Along with all this circumstantial evidence is an outstanding miracle. These persons, before their death, had for a period of time been held in the grip of a hopeless ailment; in some cases given up by the best of doctors. When raised from the dead all of them were free from their former afflictions. Herein is the overcoming power of God's hand in death.

Mrs. Anna Ward, who died, left her body on earth, ascended to the New Jerusalem in the third heaven, returned to earth, and reluctantly re-entered her body where, in Holy Ghost-given faith, her friends prayed for her return to life.

We have, then, the testimony of eye-witnesses by those who have died and gone to heaven to corroborate what others in the Spirit have also seen in vision. I know of no better or stronger proof possible, save for you and me to die and go to Paradise ourselves. Since that awaits a future day let us together look beyond the veil and pray together that the Holy Spirit will impress upon our minds the following visions of the land of realities which we shall behold when we, too, pass over the valley of death.

To recapitulate, we can be assured that what is presented in this volume, based on visions, are reliable revelation. of true realities, because:

1. Visions given by God, as recorded in the Bible, were considered as reliable as any facts of visible life.

2. Visions were to continue throughout the Church age.

3. The Lord's revelations are progressive.

4. Such visions as recorded in this book would not come from Satan.

5. These visions and revelations are not of human origin.

6. These visions themselves claim to be revelations from God to man.

7. Those seeing visions believed they saw realities.

8. The fruits resulting from these visions were divine.

9. The perfect checking of these visions with the Bible proves all to be of the same origin as the Bible—all from God.

10. Furthermore, the perfect agreement with one another as with the Bible of so many visions in so many hundreds of details shows them to be divine.

11. Persons while in vision seeing the things in heaven, or in hell, saw others who died at that exact time enter these realms.

12. In visions of Paradise and of the New Jerusalem friends and relatives who had previously died were frequently seen in spiritual, glorified bodies among the hosts of the redeemed saints in heaven.

13. The testimony of persons raised from the dead corroborates these visions.

VISIONS!

In vision and in other ways,
God spake to man from his first days;
In early Eden, with his God,
Man walked with Him on earthly sod.

And from the days of Man's first sin,
God's Spirit still did enter in
The prophet and the seer of old,
And unto them His will He told.

He talked to Moses face to face,
A chosen vessel of His grace;
And prophets, too, in vision clear,

Unto the Lord were thus made near.

In vision by the Spirit caught
They unto heaven itself were brought
To prophesy the things they saw,
As sure and certain as God's law.

They saw the Future as a Now,
Although they could not tell the How!
In early Church, by visions, still
The Lord revealed His work and will.

That visions are for all the age
Is stated clear on Sacred Page:
Which can be counted on as true,
Revealing things of Earth—made new!

And persons raised up from the dead
Repeat the things in vision said,
And what they saw while they were gone
Can always be depended on.

CHAPTER 2
THE NEW JERUSALEM, THE NEW EARTH
AND THE ULTIMATE KINGDOM

The New Jerusalem and the Throne of God

Highest of all and over all is the New Jerusalem. It is highest in the highest heaven, the Third Heaven, to which Paul was caught up. (2 Cor. 12:2). Here is the throne of God and of the Lamb, near the tree of life, in the midst of Paradise (Rev. 22).

Since God is from everlasting to everlasting and since He existed before any creation visible, or invisible, we consistently believe that His throne in the highest plain of the New Jerusalem has existed from the very beginning of any creation. May not this New Jerusalem as the setting for the throne of God have been the center from which the eternal God created the universe?

This city is also a sinless city. It will always remain a sinless city. It is an eternal city that will abide all time. It is the everlasting home of all who are redeemed by the blood of the Lamb.

A City of Light

The New Jerusalem, where Jesus reigns, is surrounded by and crowned with a glory light radiating therefrom, brighter than mortals ever see in earth's sunniest days. This is the parent city whose Creator is the Great Light that lighted all the suns and moons and stars and planets. He is the source of all light. His central city, the capital of the universe, radiates not only visible light illuminating the whole universe, but also light that endues with life every man coming into the world (John 1:9).

Through visions and reliable revelations we learn this: When saints from earth, escorted by angelic guides, approach this great city of God, having passed the suns and stars in their rapid ascent, they see in the far distance the glowing, vibrating and living glory light that surrounds and crowns this glory city.

A nearer approach to the city reveals to the amazed wonder of the new arrival the enchanting beauty of the unrivalled colored

lights sparkling from the jewel-bedecked, precious stone foundations of the walls of this light radiating jasper city.

The New Jerusalem, the
crown of creation, is in the Third
heaven. The First heaven is
above the earth and the solar
system.

The second heaven is the
starry heaven, according to revelations and visions.

John saw that: "The city lieth foursquare and the length is as
long as the breadth—the length and the breadth and the height of it
are equal", fifteen hundred miles long, fifteen hundred miles wide
and fifteen hundred miles high. "And the foundations of the wall
were garnished with all manner of precious stones", jasper (red and
yellow), sapphire (blue), chalcedony (white), emerald (yellow and
green), sardonyx (various colors), sardius (apple green), chryso-
prasus (yellowish green), chrysolyte (greenish), beryl (bluish
green), topaz (transparent white), jacinth (red), and amethyst (violet
or purple).

"The city had no need of the sun, neither of the moon to shine in
it: for the glory of God did lighten it, and the Lamb is the light
thereof." "The gates of it shall not be shut by day; for there shall be
no night there." "And the street of the city was pure gold." (Rev.
21).

Since heavenly measures cannot be estimated in earthly terms,
the dimensions of the heavenly city may far exceed anything that
can be actually expressed in terms of earthly cubits, furlongs and
miles. It is a "great city" of God whose dimensions God alone can
measure. If, however, these be earthly measurements, on every side
of the city radiates fifteen hundred miles of glittering splendor. The
jasper light walls with their twelve foundations of precious stones,

each of marvelous size, add to all its hues of jewel gleams far exceeding any rainbow aurora of earth's jewel, or Neonian displays.

A few years ago I visited Shanghai in connection with the printing of *The Three Worlds*. In that book I had tried in my imperfect way to describe the enravishing beauty of the jeweled lights of every hue shimmering from the wall of the city of God.

At the time of my visit Shanghai was called the City of Neon Lights. After living many years in the interior of China, Shanghai was to me a city of heavenly wonders. For the first time I looked upon the neon lights of various colors that embellished the streets and buildings of that city. Often did I find myself standing in the busy streets gazing with entranced wonder at those beautiful lights. Although I was in the midst of hurrying, crowding traffic, I was not of it. My mind, at any rate, was caught up to the New Jerusalem.

If those sparkling, multi-colored lights on earthly streets and buildings so entranced me, what will it be like when I behold the wonders of the city whose foundations God has laid in jewels glittering with colored lights of every shade and hue?

Within the pearly gates on streets of gold how could one stand gazing with mortal eye upon the rainbow radiance of the glory lights reflected from above into the transparent streets, or how could eye be strong enough to behold the living beams darting through the flowering trees from the gemmed mansions in the Eden parks?

Alighting one night from a street car in Shanghai, I stood for a time marveling at the beauty of the red and green and blue and yellow resplendent neon lights on the buildings before me. As we passed by I spoke of the wonder of the lights. "Yes", my companion said, "I, too, marvel; but not so much at the lights as at the expression on your face as you gazed in such enraptured admiration."

What will our wonder be when with angelic companions we first behold the glories of the city of light, the city of gold with its jeweled walls and gem-bedecked radiance, in the city of God in the highest skies—the New Jerusalem?

Paradise

That there is a Paradise in the New Jerusalem is clearly taught in the Bible, for the Spirit saith unto the churches: "To him that overcometh will I give to eat of the tree of life which is in the midst of the Paradise of God." (Rev.2:7).

In fact, the throne of God is in a Paradise, for it is in the same place as the "tree of life", that is, "in the midst of the Paradise of God." God wants us to know that His throne is in a Paradise for He told John to write a book and send to the churches all that was shown him (Rev. 1:11). Writing what the Lord told him to write and "send to the churches", John wrote: "He showed me a pure river of water, clear as crystal, proceeding out of the throne of God and of the Lamb. In the midst of the street and on either side of the river was the tree of life ("which is in the midst of the Paradise of God"), which bore twelve manner of fruit." (Rev. 22:1, 2).

The throne of God is in a Paradise. From the throne flows "a pure river of water of life, clear as crystal." On either side of the river are trees "which bear twelve manner of fruits", and beyond these are the two sections of the divided golden street of untold expanse. (Rev. 22:1,3).

The picture here is evidently not only one tree with one trunk, for it is on both sides of the river of life and bears twelve kinds of fruit. The expression "tree of life" apparently is a general term such as we commonly use when we say, "the pear", or "the peach." The beautiful picture of this Paradise is that of the river of life, clear as crystal, flowing from the throne of God and increasing and branching in its flow to water every part of this Eden and its Eastern Garden of God, the most beautiful of all the paradises in the plains of the celestial city. On either side of this beautiful river are broad boulevards of floral grandeur, and fruit trees, in fragrant bloom, bearing fruits. Back from these boulevards, on either side, must be the Edenic Splendors constituting this Paradise, for the "tree of life" is "in the midst of the Paradise of God."

The order of the river, street and Paradise must be as it reads in Weymouth's translation of the New Testament: "Then he showed me the river of the water of life, bright as crystal, issuing from the throne of God and of the Lamb. On either side of the river, midway between it and the main street was the Tree of Life. It produced twelve kinds of fruit.11 This paradisiacal order accords with the vision of Talmage when he saw saints who had been among the untalented of earth dwelling in the New Jerusalem in glorious mansions "fronting on the King's park and a back lawn sloping to the river, clear as crystal." In any case, these verses of Scripture teach that about the throne of God there is a Paradise with golden streets, rivers of water and trees bearing many kinds of fruit.

Man began in a Paradise in Eden, the garden of God. This was the Lord's first perfect order in which the human race began its infancy. When the human race reaches perfection it will again be in a Paradise of a still higher order where man will once more walk and talk with God.

The words "Eden", "Paradise", "Garden of God" are synonymous. In every instance where any of these terms are used in the Bible it means a glorious park-like condition with fruit-bearing trees, flowers, birds, animals, pools and all that goes to make an Eden.

The New Jerusalem and All Therein a Spiritual Order

The first Eden and all the first earth were earthly and on the natural flesh order, though perfect. The heavenly Eden is a higher, a spiritual, order. The New Jerusalem, with its Eden-parks and mansions, is all of the highest, the spiritual sphere.

Christ is a type of these two spheres, the earthly and the heavenly, the natural and the spiritual. When He was on earth before His resurrection Jesus was a perfect man in the likeness of the first Adam; but in His earthly life Jesus was in the flesh, the natural. After his resurrection He had a spiritual body, a heavenly body of the heavenly order; although the body of Jesus before and after His resurrection was much the same, in some ways there were differences, His spiritual body far surpassing His natural or fleshly body. For instance, Jesus could appear at once in the midst of His disciples when the doors were shut. (John 20). He could also appear in His resurrected body to walk and talk with His disciples, and at once disappear. (Luke 24).

Since the heavenly order is the spiritual one, the resurrected, spiritual state of Jesus applies to all that is the heavenly city—its streets, its parks, its rivers, its animals, its mansions, its saints, and its angels.

These facts do not lessen the realities of all the heavenly wonders. They show the heavenly sphere to be the highest one, a reality, not mere pictures, or figures of speech. In the City of God the saints have visible, though spiritualized real bodies, refined and free from all dross. In the parks of the heavenly city trees are trees. Fruit is fruit, though with a delicious flavor and life-quickening power no fruit on earth possesses. Flowers in heaven are real flowers. Their buds are so delicate, their petals so silken and their beauty so wonderful that a pilgrim from earth beholding for the first time these flowers in the Paradise of God will feel that never before had he seen a real flower. He had seen only copies of the realities.

The New Earth Also a Spiritual Earth

The first earth and all it contained, even before sin entered, was earthly. There will be a New Heaven and a New Earth in which dwelleth righteousness. (2 Peter 3:13). This is the spiritual, the eternal order. The New Earth will not be like the earth upon which the first Adam trod. It will he like the Eden the last Adam, the Christ, now treads. This is true because the New Jerusalem, with its Edens of paradisiacal glories, will be the capital of the New Earth when "the nations of them which are saved shall walk in the light of it; and the kings of the earth [the new earth] do bring their glory and honor into it." (Rev. 21:24).

The New Earth will, therefore, not be this old earth, this material, physical earth materially restored. How could the spiritual city, the New Jerusalem, be a harmonious part of any other than a spiritual order the same kind as itself, a spiritual New Earth?

The Bible furthermore clearly states that John saw "a New Heaven and a New Earth, for the first heaven and the first earth were passed away." (Rev. 21:1). The New Earth, therefore, will not be the former earth as it was in Adam's day, for "the former things are passed away." (Rev. 21:4). God wants us to make no mistake in this truth, for "He that sat upon the throne said, Behold I make all things new. And he said unto me "Write: For these words are faithful and true." (Rev. 21:6). What words are true? What words can be relied upon? Surely we need not be mistaken. God said it and told John to write it and asks us on the authority of Him who sits on the throne to believe it, that former things, the first order, passes away and also to believe that God will make all things new

All the foregoing considerations, together with the clear Bible statements of paradisiacal conditions in heaven, verify the declaration of all who have been caught up to heaven "in the body", or "out of the body", that they beheld Edenic wonders beyond the range of human language to describe, or human thought to imagine; but, all this, as we see, is a spiritual, or heavenly, order that will never become an earthly and material order.

When the angels rolled the stone away they rolled away the curse from all creation. Paradise, cursed by the first Adam's fall on the first earth, will become Paradise more than restored, it will become a resurrection-order Paradise on the New Earth, through the resurrection-redemption of Christ. "The creature (creation) itself also shall be delivered from the bondage of corruption into the glorious liberty of the children of God." (Romans 8:21)

The New Jerusalem Both First and Last

The New Jerusalem and the New Earth are not "after thoughts" of God, not a kind of second plan because man failed, thus thwarting God's purpose. Far from it. God's works were known to Him from the beginning, and all His purposes will at last be carried out.

God must have made the first earth with its Edenic wonders after creating Paradise in heaven, for was not God and His throne and His Paradise with its tree of life and its river of living water existent before Adam, or the physical earth?

Is it not true, as revealed to heavenly visitors, that in its Edenic perfection in the days of the first unfallen Adam, this present earth was God's plan for the human race in its infancy; a kindergarten for man, a starting place for the race, in truth a connected unit with the First Heaven? it was a place for man to begin the life that was to end in a still better and higher state of which earth was but a duplicate pattern in lesser glory, say our "cloud of witnesses" by revelation.

God created man in His own image: male and female created He them. And the Lord planted a garden eastward in Eden; and there He put the man whom He had formed. (Gen. 1:28; 2: 8)

God's first family was a perfect family in perfect Eden on earth. His last family will be the perfect family of the redeemed in perfect Eden in heaven.

The first earth was made by the hand of God, copied after the heavenly pattern. It was the predecessor of man's final estate on the New Earth. Since the present earth is a fallen wreck of the first perfect earth that was later destroyed by the flood, it follows that our earth today still contains perverted shadows of the perfect earth that was destroyed, and it also has a foretaste of the perfect order of the New Jerusalem. Our present world looks backward to the one that perished. At the same time it looks forward to the New Jerusalem and the New Earth that will forever remain.

Ultimate Redemption

Jesus' ultimate redemption is the deliverance and transformation of the whole creation out of its physical order into a spiritual and eternal order. Jesus is the first-born of all creation. (Col. 1: 15).

"The creation itself will be set free from its bondage to decay and obtain the glorious liberty of the children of God." This "liberty of the children of God" is none other than that for which we "groan inwardly as we wait for our adoption as sons, the redemption of the body." (Rom. 8:21-23). In other words, "the whole creation" has been groaning for the day of its liberation and transformation into the new, higher, spiritual and eternal order, the same realm for which we groan and hope, the day of release into the final resurrected spiritual world. Then mortal will put on immortality, the physical will put on the spiritual. This final order thus will apply not only to man, but also to all creation: the tree and plant and flower creation, the animal creation including all creeping things, and the whole physical and material creation of this present earth. This is the liberty the Bible assures us that is promised to the children of God and to everything in this material, natural, present earth.

Jesus, the "first fruit", the first of this new order of the physical transformed into the spiritual, will ultimately deliver all into the same realm in the day of the latter fruits, the final harvest. Therefore, the New Jerusalem of the spiritual and eternal order and the New Earth that shall be are the ultimate redemption in Jesus.

All this clear teaching of Scripture is a sufficient outline of God's revealed purpose and it is inclusive enough in its embrace to take in all the more detailed revelations we shall set forth in the following chapters of this book. These later revelations, through God-given visions, seem to be the hand of the Lord completing the picture by filling in the outline already sketched in the Word of the Lord concerning the New Jerusalem, and the New Earth, and the ultimate kingdom. (Rev. 21).

In Jesus we see God's order for all creation — the first perfect earth and its Paradise and the New Earth with its Paradise. Before His death Jesus' body was sinless, but nevertheless, natural, earthly, physical. After His resurrection His body was eternally real, but of a spiritual and higher order. So shall it be for all creation because in Jesus "all things consist" and He is "the first-born of every creature." (Col. 1:15).

THE HEAVENLY JERUSALEM

There's a city in heaven far higher than air,
The highest of all God Almighty hath made;
Where He sits on His throne, on the Holy Hill there
In Eden, where sin never cast any shade.

The river of life from the throne of God flows
With Paradise-parks by the streets, by its shore;
Where fruit in abundance, on verdant tree, grows
In perfection and order that lasts ever more.

This city of God, in His infinite plan,
Is the final abode of the once finite man;
It's a city of light and a city of love,
The peak of creation far up above.

All suns and all worlds and all that exists,
Where all life and all glory in Jesus consists:
Where Christ, in redeeming what fell in the fall,
Has become, for the universe, All that's in all.

The plains and the mansions, within jasper wall,
Converge in their order to God on His throne:
Where Father and Son and the Spirit are all
Of the life that exists, and the Three are but One.

The streets are of gold, within jasper wall
That radiates, everywhere, jasper-like light
To lighten the heavens and permeate all,
With glory that's mellow and never too bright.

Its jeweled foundations and gemmed mansions, too,
Are parts of the order of our Savior's plan
For His city to rule over all to be new,
When His work is complete in redeeming lost man.

CHAPTER 3
THE NEW JERUSALEM
(Continued)

Paradisiacal Plains in the New Jerusalem

According to visions repeatedly seen by different persons the New Jerusalem is a series of paradisiacal plains one above another. Each plain is in itself a heavenly city with its homes and centers of instruction and its rivers and in numerable series of paradise- parks.

Although everyone of these city - paradise - plains is of a glory surpassing the highest conceptions of mortals, these plains are, nevertheless, arranged in ascending degrees of grandeur, the most magnificent and glorious being the highest plain wherein is the throne of God in the midst of the most resplendent paradise of all.

Just how many plains constitute this city of God we do not know. Marietta Davis, after visiting much of the plain of the Infants' Paradise, was by angelic guidance escorted to see spiritual views of higher plains, up to the seventh degree above, or evidently the seventh higher plain. Sundar Singh also repeatedly saw these plains in the New Jerusalem; but, whether these series of heavenly plains in the New Jerusalem are only seven in number, or more, or additional series of sevens, no one seems to have seen. That there are at least seven plains we know by these revelations. Of course, we know that God, who suspends worlds in space, can just as easily suspend a paradise - city plain anywhere.

Whether this city of God is in the form of a pyramid, or that of a cube, does not appear to have been clearly revealed. Since the Bible says that: "the city lieth four square, and the length and the breadth and the height of it are equal", we see that so far as this description reveals, the city might be either a cube, or a pyramid.

Bible students have quite generally supposed the city must be a pyramid because this seemed to be the only natural explanation that would answer the question as to how such a city could be as high as it is long and wide. With this revelation of the series of heavenly plains, however, it becomes evident that the city of God could as well be cubical and still accord with the Bible's limited and partial description. This does not, on the contrary, forbid the possibility of the city's being pyramidal in form, the highest plain being that of least expansion and the largest plain being the lowest. Some revelations gave that impression, but these were not in sufficiently clear outline to make it positive that the celestial city is in fact pyramidal.

The Paradisiacal Order

The various plains of the golden city are similar in appearance, though varying in details and differing in beauty and glory, as already stated. We have a clear revelation of the heavenly arrangement of the Infants' Plain where babies are nurtured and cared for. This Infants' Plain is much the same as those seen by other visitors to other plains of the city. On the Infants' Paradisiacal Plain in this holy city the arrangement is one of wonderful symmetry and heavenly perfection. The order revealed is as follows:

A magnificent temple of worship and instruction, with which no structures on earth can be compared in dimensions or grandeur, forms a dome-like glory crown at the more elevated apex of the whole paradisiacal plain.

This central temple is surrounded by Edenic beauties. Wide stretches of velvety lawns, clumps of trees with beautiful foliage and fragrant flowers abound. Trees with life invigorating, delicious fruits also abound, while of flowering shrubs and blossoming vines there seems to be no end. By each pebbled, or marbled, or golden walk, flowers of every hue, sprinkled in the ever-verdant turf everywhere abounding, lift their fragrant faces. Scriptural beauty in marble, white, or in varied tints, and fountains tinged with gold are scattered here and there.

Birds of every plume and size flit from bough to bough, each singing its own joyous song of praise, yet all in one concordant harmony. Beneath the trees animal pets of every kind frolic in their perfect love. (Rev. 21:-1 44. Matt. 17).

In Eden, in heaven, trees are trees, flowers are flowers, homes are homes. They are all of a higher order than ever was the earthly — Eden, perfect order. They are spiritual. "That was not first which is spiritual, but that which is natural; and afterward that which is spiritual." (1 Cor. 15:46).

From Glory to Glory

The central temple of each plain forms the glory-peak of the plain. It is the most magnificent of all those on its plain and is located at the top and center of the plain which from every side descends in easy and graceful undulations. From the groups of the central temple flows a life-giving river, increasing as it flows, carrying its waters to every part of the whole paradise-park. This transparent, crystal river with source at the central temple in the middle of the plain, after gently descending a short distance, flows around the central dome in a spiral way, making circle after circle as it descends the plain, in all making twelve complete circles, the first circle being the smallest about the central temple and the last circle being one of greatest diameter near the outer borders of the plain. In this way the plain is transversely intersected twelve times by the spiral river of gently flowing water.

This spiral river is bordered on either side by a beautiful golden avenue with trees, shrubs and flowers. From the outer edge of the plain twelve golden streets, or boulevards, gradually ascend from all sides to the central palace where all streets converge.

In this way, by the twelve circles of the avenue-bordered river and the twelve intersecting boulevards the plain is divided into one hundred and forty-four wards, each bounded on the upper and lower sides by the river of life, and on the other two sides by the golden boulevards. It is apparent that bridges of beautiful architecture must cross the crystal waters at each intersection of boulevards and golden streets at every corner of each ward.

On either side of the boulevards and river are paradise-like conditioned where, as far as eye can see, are scenes of beauty in over verdant trees of all designs of beautiful foliage and trunks of various hues. Open stretches of grass as soft as silk, and beds of flowers in every shade are only parts of this wondrous park. Fragrance from flowers of every kind perfumes the air at every turn. Never on this earth has been such beauty in fern and flower, nor ever has bloomed such fragrant rose, declare those who have seen the heavenly parks. The fruits growing on every hand are of a finer flavor than mortals ever tasted, and they have a life-invigorating power adapted to heaven.

In each of the one hundred and forty-four wards every palace is in its own park of edenic arrangement and beauty. Palace after palace is systematically located at a distance from each boulevard and avenue-bordered river.

Since the descriptions of these temples, or infants' nurseries, as seen by Marietta Davis, are given in *The Three Worlds* it is unnecessary to repeat here in full. Yet for those who may not have read the book, much of the description of the Infants' Paradise is here repeated. (Rev. 21:4 46. Rev. 4:5).

A river of pure water, clear as crystal, flows from the central palace of instruction on the infants' paradisiacal plain and flows around it in twelve increasing spiral circles to the outer border of the plain. On either side are borders of edenic avenues and beyond are temples of instruction surrounded by Paradise grandeur.

These one hundred and forty-four wards, or Eden parks, increase in beauty. The outer row of twelve wards between the eleventh and twelfth circles of the river are the lowest both in position and in paradisiacal adornment. The series in the next circle have added loveliness; the ones within the next higher circle have increasing splendor; and so on, so that each of the twelve circles of paradise-wards increases in beauty up to the climax of all in the most beautiful central ward in the highest circle with its central temple.

The placement of palace homes within each of the one hundred and forty-four wards is also varied. The temples, or palaces of instruction in the outer circle of wards is the lowest in rank with varying degrees of beauty among the temples within the ward itself. The temples within each rank within each circle of wards are all of greater sculptural magnificence than the finest in the circle below. Thus all the temples in the wards of all the heavenly plains differ in increasing grandeur, ranging from the most remote to the centermost palace, the most beautiful one in the ward.

Though differing in arrangement and splendor, all of the parks and all of the temples in each of the one hundred and forty-four wards are but smaller patterns of the great central ward and the central temple in that park. The whole plain thus forms one harmonized system.

According to vision, and in harmony with Scripture, all of the other heavenly plains, in turn, are alike in one respect: All are traversed by rivers and golden streets running through paradise-parks, the streets converging from all parts of each plain to the central park where there is the central edifice of the highest order on each respective and separate plain. This agreement is on general lines; that is, each plain is a plain of paradise-parks with corresponding arrangement of golden avenues and crystal rivers. In the parks are situated temples, mansions and edifices for instruction.

But, aside from these general similarities, the Eden-parks in heaven are of endless variety and degrees of splendor. As on earth, for example, each city has a number of parks, yet they differ one from another both in arrangement and beauty. The parks in one city, in turn, differ from those in another city.

The Infants' Paradise

On the plain where infants from earth are first nurtured and trained are one hundred and forty-four wards, as already stated, and in each ward are fifty-seven mansions, or infants' homes, each one in an Eden-like park of its own. The homes differ in style of architecture as the parks around them differ in arrangement and beauty.

Hence, in one ward are fifty-seven paradise-parks and on this one plain of one hundred and forty-four wards there are eight thousand five hundred and eight distinct, and in some way separated parks, or lesser Edens. Few, if any of these, are alike. Each park is the special one harmoniously suited to the one edifice in that park.

In detail the plains differ one from the other in ascending order. On some are mountains and valleys and level plains. There are rolling lawn-like stretches of green like spacious golf links. Of such scenic splendors there is greater variety than we find on earth, a thousand times more beautiful than the marvels of which we see but dim, imperfect reflections in the best of earthly parks.

What Eye-Witnesses Saw

One who was caught up to heaven attempts to describe a beautiful lake seen in the glory-light of one paradisiacal plain. She says: "I caught my breath, then stopped abruptly and covered my face with my hands to shield my eyes from the glorified scene. No wonder that my brother had not brought me to this place; I was scarcely yet spiritually strong enough to look upon it. When I again slowly lifted my head Mae was standing like one entranced. The golden light rested upon her face, and mingling with the radiance that had birth within, almost transfigured her. Even she, so long an inhabitant here (in heaven), had not yet grown accustomed to the glory. 'Look, Auntie! It is God's will that you should see', she softly whispered, not once turning her eyes away from the scene before her. 'He allowed me to be the one to show you the glory of this place.'

One Caught Up to Paradise, writes: "I turned and looked like one half awakened. Before us spread a lake as smooth as glass, but flooded with golden glory caught from the heavens, that made it like a sea of molten gold. The blossom and fruit-bearing trees grew down to its very border in many places." (W.P. 60)

"I turned and looked like one but half awakened. Before us spread a lake as smooth as glass, but flooded with a golden glory caught from the heavens that made it like a sea of molten gold. The blossom and fruit-bearing trees grew down to its very border in many places, and far, far away across the shining waters arose the domes and spires of what seemed to be a mighty city. Many people were resting upon the flowery banks, and on the surface of the water were boats of wonderful structure, filled with happy souls, and propelled by an unseen power. Little children, as well as grown-up persons, were floating upon, or swimming in, the water; and as we looked a band of singing cherubs floating high overhead, drifted across the lake, their baby voices borne to us where we stood, in notes of joyful praise.18

"'Glory and honor', sang the child voices.

"'Dominion and power', caught up and answered the voices of the vast multitude together; and in the strain I found that Mae and I were joining. The cherub band floated onward, and away in the distance we caught the faint melody of their sweet voices and the stronger cadence of the response from those waiting below.

"We stood upon the margin of the lake, and my cheeks were tear bedewed and my eyes dim with emotion. I felt weak as a little child; but, oh, what rapture, what joy unspeakable filled and overwhelmed me—groups of children played around in joyous freedom. Some climbed the trees that overhung the water with agility of squirrels, and disappeared with happy shouts of laughter into the lake, floating around upon its surface like immense and beautiful water-lilies or lotus flowers.

"No fear of harm or danger; no dread of ill, or anxiety lest a mishap occur; security and joy and peace!

"'This is, indeed, a blessed life', I said, as we stood watching the sports of happy children" (Quoted from Intro Murros).

As the paradisiacal beauty of the plains grade from the lowest to the highest plain, and from the most remote ward to the paradise of

God in the highest sphere, the grandeur of the sculptural excellence of the temples is also in ascending magnificence. The sculptural beauty of even the most remote ward and the lowest temples, both in dimensions and embellishments, is far beyond anything mortals have ever seen and beyond any power of human language to describe.

In other words, the most beautiful of man's parks with their nooks and dells and flowering vines and shrubs, their trickling streams, their lakes and crystal pools, their winding pebbled walks beneath blossoming trees and verdant bowers, their marble fountains and granite arches—all these with a hundred added beauties wrought by human hands, are a far inferior to the lowest order of Paradise as the earth is inferior to heaven.

Likewise, it is the unvarying declaration of all who have been caught up to see the glories of the heavenly city that to describe even the temples, the schools, or the mansions, is impossible for several reasons: The heavenly buildings are spiritual, not material. Though similar to earthly buildings they are different. Many are of such vast dimensions they have no comparison with structures on earth. Then again, the beauty of these heavenly buildings is incomparable. They appear as if made of marble, granite, rare wood, gold, silver, diamonds and other jewels of amazing size, together with a thousand adornments never seen by man, and all of such surpassing elegance that no human words can picture it.

Of that heavenly land as seen by General Booth he wrote: "No human eyes ever beheld such perfection, such beauty. No earthly ear ever heard such music. No human heart ever experienced such ecstasy as it was my privilege to see, hear and feel in the celestial country. Around me was an atmosphere so balmy that it made my whole frame vibrate with pleasure. The bank of roses on which I found myself reposing had, flowing by it, the waters of the clearest, purest river that seemed to dance with delight to its own murmurings. The trees that grew upon the banks were covered with the greenest foliage, and laden with most delicious fruit—sweet beyond all earthly sweetness—and by lifting my hand I could pluck and taste; while in every direction above and around me the whole air seemed to be laden with sweetest odors coming from the fairest flowers."

Another witness describes a heavenly scene as "infinitely exceeding in beauty and splendor the most elevated conception of mortals, a place whose glories no language could describe." As another witness was walking along an avenue of the celestial city she noticed that "the streets were made of highly polished gold which shone brighter than the sun on earth. The large, beautiful mansions were made of all the jewels that were ever visible in this world below. These magnificent mansions were more wondrous than king's palaces. Little children were dancing and playing. All were rejoicing in their Savior.

"The air was filled with the sweet perfume of the flowers. Birds were singing gaily, and little brooks tinkled merrily through ferns, flowers and trees. Everyone and everything were praising and exalting God. After walking for a while we came to a gorgeous palace. My eyes were blinded for a moment at its grandeur."

Truly, "eye hath not seen, nor ear heard, neither hath entered into the heart of man the things which God hath prepared for them that love Him." (1 Cor.2:9).

In summary then, the New Jerusalem in the third heaven as we have seen, is a series of paradisiacal plains one above another in ascending magnificence. The plain of superlative glory, the highest, is the plain in which is the throne of God, and from which flows the river of pure water into the paradisiacal parks that surround the mansions of the redeemed. (Rom. 8:21-23 48. II. Cor. 3:18).

More or less deeply buried in the hearts of men is appreciation of the Paradise lost. Unconsciously they restore in part beauties that, through Christ, will be restored in full.

IN PARADISE

On heaven's plains, both high and low,
Where crystal waters always flow:
In robes and garments white as snow,
The saints of ages come and go.

And in the air that's always clear
The angels everywhere appear;
Singing praises to the King.
Their anthems make all heaven ring
As they soar and float away
Through eternal, nightless day.

All the parks in heaven's sky
Are filled with praise to God on high;
Where carols in a chorus rise,

As joined by all plains in the skies.

The birds and beasts all have a part,
And shrubs and flowers and roe and hart;
And palms and branches of the trees
All join in heaven's jubilees.

The angels floating in the sky,
And saints with harps and trumpets nigh;
The Spirit moves to one great hymn
In which each saint can enter in?
With chords too fine for mortal ears
To sing with heart now free from tears.

One Spirit moves all everywhere,
In air and park and mansions there;
At intervals, as in one voice,
To praise their Lord—in Him rejoice!

CHAPTER 4
THE HEAVENLY PLAINS

The Plains Surround the New Jerusalem

While the New Jerusalem is clearly revealed as being a series of heavenly plains, such paradisiacal plains are not confined to those within the city itself. One very remarkable revelation in vision by a person caught up to the Third Heaven shows that wonderful Paradise-plains extend without the gates of the golden city in unknown expanse. The grandeur of these plains without the city was scarcely less than that within the gates, making this great outside plain a world in itself with the New Jerusalem in its center. More about this plain without and surrounding the city of God will be added in a later chapter and volume.

Plains in the Third Heaven Below the New Jerusalem

Sundar Singh and Marietta Davis and others who had visions and revelations of the heavenly order, though with out knowing about each other's visions, agree that below the heavenly city that is highest in the Third Heaven, there are other paradise-city plains. These lower plains below the New Jerusalem, according to these visions, are like the glorious plains within the city of God.

Like the heavenly plains within the city, these plains below it in the Third Heaven are in series, the higher the plain the more resplendent and wonderful in paradisiacal grandeur. All are of the sinless New Jerusalem glory, but as plains ascend in series they increase in paradisiacal variation and glories, no two exactly alike, yet all one coordinate united whole.

The first earth, when perfect, was a lower reflection of the higher order in high heavens.

To no one, as far as I know, has been revealed the number of plains in these series in the Third Heaven. It was more than once revealed to many persons that there is, however, the Third Heaven distinct from the Second Heaven, and that the Third Heaven, with its New Jerusalem, is above and beyond the starry heaven, which is the Second Heaven.

The Bible definitely speaks of the Third Heaven, thereby establishing the truth of a Second Heaven and of a First Heaven. It was the belief of the Jews that the Third Heaven is above the starry heaven. This, as we see, agrees with what is now revealed through the Spirit of the Lord to His children.

More about the Third Heaven will be discussed in sub sequent chapters.

Paradisiacal Plains in the Second Heaven

Sundar Singh, Marietta Davis and others independent of one another saw in revelation that the Second Heaven is the "starry heaven" and that this Second Heaven, like the Third Heaven and its New Jerusalem, is a series of paradise plains. Here again, as in the case of the highest heaven, or Third Heaven, the plains in the second Heaven are arranged in series of ascending grandeur, the most glorious being the highest of these plains.

More about these plains in the Second Heaven will be found in later chapters of this book and in another volume.

Paradisiacal Plains in the First Heaven

The First Heaven, as shown by many revelations, is the heaven below the "starry heaven." It is the heaven above the earth, and it includes the heaven of our atmosphere. This agrees with the belief of the Jews, although of the persons receiving these revelations few, if any, knew this. Since Israel, as God's chosen people in the past, had constant revelations direct from Him, we have good reason to believe that what they held to be true on such questions as we are discussing had some basis in supernatural revelation.

According to many revelations through visions and in other ways, Sundar Singh, especially, saw that as created in the beginning, the First Heaven, like the Second Heaven and the Third Heaven above it, was created a series of paradisiacal plains. These paradise-plains in the First Heaven, as in the case of those in the higher heavens, were, like those above, arranged in series of ascending beauty and magnificence. Every plain was a scene of unsurpassing varieties and entrancing wonders. Yet glorious as was even the lowest plain of these paradise-marvels, each plain in ascending resplendence exceeded the plain immediately below it. These paradise-plains as they came from the hand of God descended in their paradisiacal wonders right down to the primordial earth itself.

The present condition and the inhabitants of the plains in the First Heaven will be discussed in other chapters and in another volume.

The Primordial Paradise Earth and Its Order

When God created the earth it was perfect and without sin. It was also a paradise-order, as the Bible clearly reveals. The written Word of God also reveals that this primordial earth was not only of a paradise-order, but was also, like the heavens above it a series of paradise-wonders. We see this in the fact that after the Lord had made all the earth "very good" with all of its floral and fauna wonders, a whole paradise-world, he made also the Garden of Eden with more than usual magnificence. Within this Eden He placed man, the climax of His earthly creation, in a more exceedingly beautiful garden within a garden. (Heb. 1:8,10). We see, then, that in the beginning, the paradise-earth itself was a series of paradise-wonders.

This condition of the primordial earth is discussed more fully in my book, *The Three Worlds*. The present condition of the earth and its inhabitants is also dealt with in that volume and in later chapters of this book and in another volume.

All One Original Unity

From what has been written it is apparent, therefore, that before sin entered, the earth and the First Heaven and the Second Heaven and the Third Heaven and the New Jerusalem were all in series of paradisiacal glories.

According to these revelations we further see that the earth in the beginning was in series of ascending wonders, and we see that the First Heaven above it was a series of paradise-plains in series of ascending grandeurs. The Second and Third Heavens, in turn, were a still more magnificent series of parasidiacal city plains in ascending splendors, and finally, the New Jerusalem on the highest plain in the Third and highest Heaven, is a magnificent city of paradisiacal resplendence that arises from heaven's highest plain as a city of plains, one plain above another, like a series of parasidiacal cities, or city-plains, one above another.

THERE ARE THREE HEAVENS

The First heaven surrounds the earth; the Second heaven is the realm of the stars; the Third Heaven is above all else. Every heaven has a series of vast paradisiacal plains. These increase in paradisical splendors in ascending order. The New Jerusalem, the heavenly city, is on the highest plain in the Third heaven, within it are also paradisiacal plains in ascending order.

This heavenly city is, according to the Bible, about 1500 miles square and 1500 miles high. Each plain in the New Jerusalem would be, then, as extensive as the United States. How many such successive plains are in that 1500 miles upward series no man knows.

Still other plains extend outside the gates of the heavenly city in great expanse. When we consider all this, together with the fact of the great number of vast plains in the Second heaven and those in the First heaven, we see that the countries and kingdoms of our earth would appear very small compared with the paradisiacal plains in the heavens and the kingdom of God.

This City of God, this city of golden streets and mansions and splendors is the "crown-city" of all the plains on earth and in all of the heavens, the city in which is the throne of God and of the Lamb whence comes all the light and all the life of all the cities and all the heavens and all the paradise wonders on all the plains and on earth.

All the splendors on all the plains in all the heavens are descending copies of the greatest glory on the highest plain in the highest heaven on the highest plain in the New Jerusalem whence all beauties and glories descend.

While similar and yet different, the order in all the heavens is spiritual, and that on the earth is physical, natural and earthly.

All of this, the unified relationship of all in the beginning, and that of the present aspect of heaven's plains is further discussed in my book, The Three Worlds, and in later chapters that follow in this book and in another volume.

Earth's parks are but pictures of the glorious real spiritual parks on heaven's plains.

PLAINS OF THE FIRST HEAVEN

Plains, and plains, and higher plains
In all the heavens' vast domains:
In Heavens First, and Second, Third,
Exceeding all that man has heard.

In Heaven First the plains were placed,
So that these plains the earth embraced;
Angelic hosts from God above,
Dwelt on these plains in perfect love.
Each plain a paradise of peace,
Was one of series to increase
In work and wonders of the Lord,
Created thus by His own Word.

The perfect earth, as it was made,
Reclined in peace beneath the shade
Of plains above, whose glory then
Was part of earth and knew no sin.

A perfect part of perfect plan,
Were plains and earth as made for man:
Where Eden plains and earth should be
All parts of one great harmony.

This earth, with Paradise complete,
Was placed at Adam's perfect feet
With plains of God in heaven above:
One in Spirit, one in love.

The perfect man, in perfect grace,
Could higher go from place to place;
From plain to plain above the earth—
From earthly into heavenly birth.

SECOND AND THIRD HEAVENS' PLAINS

The Second Heaven is the sky,
And many million miles on high;
Where moon and sun and stars appear,
Beyond all comprehension here.

These plains, whose number men don't know,
Each grander than the one below;
In paradises' wonders lay,
In harmonies' eternal day.

The bounds and borders of each plain
Enclose an untold vast domain:
With jeweled homes on golden street,
Where man may dwell and angels meet.

As he ascends from plain to plain,
From Adam's earth, his first domain,
Unto the city of His God,
The place to be his last abode.

It's earthly first and heavenly last,
And man must go from class to class;
From natural into Spiritual birth,
To progress in accord with worth.

The highest are the heavens
Third, As clearly stated in the Word;
In series, too, where plain on plain
Increase in splendors here again.

Unto the city that has plains,
Where God, on highest one, now reigns
And Christ, forever shall be King,
Where earth and plains all tribute bring.

CHAPTER 5
JESUS THE LIFE OF THE NEW JERUSALEM

Jesus in Everything

The highest, or Third Heaven, is the heaven of the throne of Christ. Of the Son it is written, "Thy throne, O God, is for ever and ever", and "Thou Lord in the beginning hast laid the foundation of the earth; and the heavens are the work of Thy hands." (Luke 1:31,32).

Down from this throne in highest heaven to Bethlehem came the one to be called "Jesus", "the Son of the Highest." (Luke 1:31,32 51. Zeph. 2:3). When He humbled Himself to ride upon an ass and entered the earthly Jerusalem on His way to the deepest humiliation of the cross and the grave, the Holy Spirit inspired multitudes sang: "Blessed is He that cometh in the name of the Lord; Hosanna in the highest." (Matt. 21:9).

Out of the deepest humiliation, a rejected outcast, Christ again ascended to His throne in the highest heaven. Here He sat down on the right hand of God who had raised Him from the dead and exalted Him "far above all principality and power and might and dominion and everything that is named, not only in this world, but also in that which is to come; and hath put all things under His feet and gave Him to be the head over all things to the church, which is His body, the fullness of him that filleth all in all." (Eph. 1:20-22) While Jesus, the Christ, "filleth all in all", "and all things in Him exist", and He is in all things, at the same time He is more than all things. As a workman is more than his works, so is Christ more than all. "For by Him (Christ) were all things created that are in heaven and that are in earth, visible and invisible, whether they be thrones or dominions, or principalities, or powers, all things were created by Him and for Him; and He is before all things, and by Him all things exist. And He is the head of the body, the church; who is the beginning, the first-born from the dead: that in all things He might have the preeminence." (Col. 1:18, 19)

When Jesus, after His resurrection, ascended on high, He ascended "far above all principality and power and might and dominion, and everything that is named (in highest heavens and on earth), not only in this world, but also in that which is to come; and has put all things under His feet and gave Him to be the head over all things to the church, which is His body, the fullness of Him that filleth all in all" (Eph. 1:20-23). Thus the resurrected Christ fills all the highest heavens and all its city and all its Paradise and all the universe with Himself, in whom "all things exist" (Col. 1:17).

Throughout the reading of this book it is to be remembered that above all and in all is Jesus. There is nothing in heaven in all its glories that in any manner detracts from the glory of Jesus. All things add to His glory and are with Him harmonious parts of His redeeming grace. All heaven's perfected order and beauty exist in Christ and "for him." As J. R. Moseley loves to say through direct revelation: "Jesus is 'perfect everything.'"

The Highest of all is the Victor over death and the grave: He was and is and ever shall be; He is the head of all creation, "the first -born of every creature", "the first-born from the dead." (Col. 1:18, 19).

The life of the heavenly city is Jesus. As the light of the celestial city radiates from the throne of God and of the Lamb, so also does life proceed from the throne. In all heaven there is not a living being whose life does not pulsate with the spiritual life of Jesus.

The four living creatures about the throne of Christ and the four and twenty elders before Him live in His life. Their hearts throb with His life.

Like the "pure river of life" that flows from the throne of God and the Lamb, bringing joy and life to an in its onward and downward course to all of Paradise, the life of Jesus flows outward and downward through every plain and every New Jerusalem. Jesus' life is in all, and all are conscious of His life and presence everywhere in heaven.

The angels in heaven, living in their original glory and perfection, exist in the life of Him in whom alone there is life in the celestial realms.

The redeemed from earth, now in heaven, born again of the Holy Spirit and having discarded the encumbering body of clay live fully in the life of the Holy Spirit, which is also the life of Jesus who fills all and everyone. On earth they who are born again of the Holy Spirit have an "earnest" of the Spirit, a small down payment. At times of the baptism of the Holy Spirit and in moments of great inflows of life from above we seem to be lifted into heavenly realms to partake of the very life of Jesus. Even so, these higher experiences of men still in the flesh on earth are mere "fore-tastes" of the ecstatic joys in the full life of Jesus in the higher land of unhindered spiritual realities. The supreme joy of every saint in heaven is this life in the fullness of the resurrected Christ. This is a perfect life in His Spirit in the city of realities. Jesus in everyone, and everyone in Jesus makes heaven.

All life in Paradise is life in Jesus, pure, undefiled life where children play in the waters of life. It is in His children that enables them truly to see the Paradise without. It is Jesus in all that makes a perfect Paradise.

Filled with the life that comes from the throne, every saint in all heaven is quickened and enlightened to comprehend and appreciate the beauties of the Paradise in which he lives. Without this spiritual illumination in the life of the Spirit of Christ Paradise would not be paradise. The life of Christ within is essential to the full enjoyment of the Paradise without.

A Foretaste Now

This phase of man's relation to the paradise about him can be known in a measure while on earth. For instance, a man just saved out of a life of sin, after he goes to work the next morning after his redemption, seems like one released from prison and placed in another world. He does not remember of ever before having heard a bird so much as chirp as he passed along. Now every bush seems to hold a caroling songster whose jubilant music sounds to him like the singing of birds from Paradise. Every bird seems to out-sing the nightingale, and of variety there seems to be no end.

To this newly saved man, this born-again babe in Christ, every green bough seems to be waving praises to God in rhythm with the singing of the birds. The grass on the lawns looks like velvet swards. Every flower appears to nod to him as it joins him in praising their common Lord. Trees in the fields seem to be hands lifted in praises to God. And the growing crops of ripening grain seem to be flourishing in Eden.

Why the change in this man? The birds had always sung praises to God as morning after morning he had passes them, stumbling along stupefied from the night's carousal. The branches had always been waving a welcome to him and praises to God. In many a field ripened grain, unnoticed by him, had waved in the morning breeze as he trudged along, and the trees had always been lifting hands heavenward. But the slave to sin had been shut in a spiritual prison. Cut off from the Spirit of God, shut away from the Lord's creation, his eyes could not see beauty. No flower could he behold. His ears were dead to sound; no singing bird could he hear in his prison. Shut away from Eden, no waving fields of grain could he see. Wonder of wonders! When Jesus passed by his prison door and set him free, he was free just as Jesus had promised when He said, "The Son shall make you free and you shall be free, indeed." (John 8 :36). The difference was that the Spirit of God, the life of Jesus, had come into this new man's heart and freed him from self to behold the Eden on earth in which he really lived, but knew it not. Tuned in with God he could for the first time really see and enjoy God's Eden and sing with God's birds in earth's paradise songs which none but the Lord's own children ever sing.

To the saved out of a sinful life and filled with the Holy Spirit the Savior opens up a hitherto unnoticed Paradise all about him. To the redeemed, anointed by the Holy Spirit, every bird sings sweeter, every flower seems fresher, the air more balmy, and every blade of grass and every tree appears to be waving praise to God.

Do you know something of this man's experience? I do. At times when I have inflow from the throne of God I notice that every bird sings sweeter, every flower seems fresher, and the mountains seem more paradise-like, while the hills clap their hands for joy. Jesus' life within enables us to see and enjoy the Eden without, either on earth, or in heaven.

Jesus Everything and in Everything

The heavenly Eden is a part of this life in Jesus. Everything in Paradise is spiritually endued and quickened in Him. The birds singing carols of unending praise to Jesus are inspired by His life and spirit within them. Every bough and every leaf of verdant trees in heaven's caressing breezes waves its adoration to its Lord. The happy animals in park and pasture romp and praise the One who fills them all with His own loving nature. Flowers that bloom by the way side, flowers that bloom in the dell, and flowers on vine and tree reflect from their faces the face of Jesus and shed from their petals heavenly aromas that flow from their Lord.

The wooded hills and verdant valleys; mountains; grand and

rolling plains; birds and beasts; fern and flowers; saints and angels in the parks and in the heavenly air are all a united, harmonious whole; all live in one life of love, the life of Jesus, the All-in-All.

Jesus being in the life of all the New Jerusalem from the lowest plain to the highest, and being in every creature from the tiniest bird, or fern, or flower to saints and archangels, all heaven pulsates with the life of Jesus as one organic whole, one body.

At intervals waves of praise simultaneously sweep over the whole city and plains as if arising from a single heart. A million voices blend in one; a million palms and branches wave in rhythm. All that is animate, or that exists, in voice or vibration, are component parts of the great celestial symphony. "And I heard the voice of many angels—the number of them was ten thousand times ten thousand, and thousands of thousands, saying with a loud voice, 'worthy is the Lamb that was slain to receive power, and riches, and wisdom, and strength, and honor, and glory, and blessing. And every creature which is in heaven—heard I saying, blessing, and honor, and glory, and power be unto him that sitteth upon the throne and unto the Lamb for ever and ever.'" (Rev. 5:11-13). Here is a partial picture of the final great symphony to be joined by more than highest heaven—some day by all lower heavens—but now sung in all the city of the New Jerusalem.

To the songs of praise, adoration and worship that at intervals burst from all parts of the celestial city, from the farthest mansion to the palace of the wonderful King, are added the celestial music of harpers playing on their silver-stringed harps, and divinely inspired music of other heavenly instruments far surpassing all our world has ever heard.

Every note of every song of "every creature which is in heaven" and every touch on every harp and every sound from every other instrument are in perfect harmony in this universal heavenly symphony — not a mistaken note, not an erroneous touch in all the city of God.

Although at the seasons of spontaneous praise and adoration waves of song and music rise to the greatest volume, there is always rhythm and music in all of heaven. Like pulsations from the heart of Jesus, whence comes the life of all, everything that moves in heaven moves in rhythm. Heaven is always a rhythmic choir; even when all are serving, the measure of the tread of saints is tuned to the music in their souls.

One privileged to behold this rhythmic, harmonious movement of the heavenly life wrote: "All the orders of heaven were in perfect and blessed harmony, and appeared to be directed in all their movements by a mysterious influence proceeding from the throne of God."

The river that proceeds from the throne of God is a river of pure "water of life." Wherever it flows its waters carry life from the throne and the Lamb. In the Paradise on either side of this river are the trees of "life", bearing twelve manners of fruit, the roots of which trees are watered in this pure river that flows from the throne. In like manner all the crystal streams and rivulets and transparent pools and sparkling fountains throughout every paradise on each heavenly plain consist of "pure water of life." Like the waters that Ezekiel saw (Ezek. 47) these waters bring life in which the flowering and fruit- bearing trees of Paradise bathe their roots and from which they draw their life.

The fruits that grow on the "trees of life", in some peculiar way enlarge and nurture the life of those who partake of them. As man in the unfallen state in the first perfect Eden was to eat of "life-giving fruits" so will he in the last Eden.* As Jesus "ate and drank" with His disciples "after he arose from the dead", in heaven His disciples will again eat and drink with Him.

In the heavenly plains the animal creation to whom the Lord has given "every herb for food", grazing in the heavenly fields thereby eat and partake of the life of Jesus, the life that comes from pure waters flowing from the throne of God.

Heavenly inhabitants drinking pure, limpid waters drink "water of life" from Him who is the "living water."

Saints who bathe in glassy lakes, or crystal streams, emerge from the living water of life with a sense of new exhilaration and enlarged capacities. Here are transparent waters in whose depths a child can never drown, waters to swim in, beneath whose surface the children of the Lord may wander to gather variegated pebbles of every hue and color without fear of death.

There is, then, not a spot in the New Jerusalem that is not filled with the life of Jesus, the life of the King of the resurrection. Every flower shedding its fragrance, every bird singing from heavenly

---

* For further evidence that there will be literal eating and drinking in the kingdom of God, see *The Three Worlds*.

boughs in ecstatic joy, every young lion romping with the calf and kitten beneath spreading trees, every child playing by crystal waters, every saint praising his God in anthems divine, every angel floating in the balmy atmosphere, every creature that moves, or lives; or has its being, everything in mount or valley, or plain, or park, or mansion, everything that exists—all these live in the life of Jesus. To Him all highest heaven and all the spiritual city audibly give incessant, never-ending praise, glory, adoration, worship and service.

Flowers in heaven's Paradise send forth fragrance that is the aroma from the Lily of the Valley, and the Rose of Sharon — Jesus.

JESUS EVERYWHERE IN HEAVEN

In every flower and petal fair,
In fragrance in the air;
In verdant leaf on every tree,
And everything that eye can see,

Has share in one component part
Of life and love from Jesus' heart;
He's everything in everything,
He's in the songs the angels sing.

And in the life in all the land,
In heaven's holy strand;
Everything that lives and moves
Is always as the Lord approves.

For not a breath and not a sound,
In all of heaven can be found,
That's not a part of Jesus' power,
Every second, minute, hour.

In mansion, park, or anywhere,
The blessed Lord is always there;
He's everything: He's All-in-all,
Not one from Him will ever fall.

In every plain in heaven's land,
Whatever lives can understand
That in this life so full and free,
All shall dwell eternally.

CHAPTER 6
THE INHABITANTS OF THE NEW JERUSALEM

Old Testament History

All of God's people who have died since the days of Adam are now happy inhabitants of the New Jerusalem. This is the teaching of the Bible, for when we come to the New Jerusalem we are come to "Mount Zion and unto the city of the living God, the heavenly Jerusalem — and to the spirits of just men made perfect." (Heb. 12:22, 23).

Jesus said to the repentant thief on the cross, "Today shalt thou be with me in Paradise" (Luke 23:43). That day the dead body of the thief was on the cross. His soul was in Paradise, the Garden of God, the Eden of the Lord. This was not soul-sleeping, soul-unconsciousness. It was entrance into an enlarged life in the abundance of God's glory. It was entrance into the conscious life of eternal peace by still waters and green pastures.

In the heavenly city then are the spirits of "just men made perfect", the saved of God from the beginning of God's saving grace. Here the saints of both Old and New Testament, and the saints of all succeeding centuries unite in heaven's ways on the plains of this city of the Third Heaven. Abraham, when on earth, "sojourned in the land of promise as in a strange country, dwelling in tabernacles—for he looked for a city which hath foundations, whose builder and maker is God." (Heb. 11:9,10). Although the Lord had promised earthly possession of the land of Canaan to Abraham and his seed, he well knew that his real Canaan was the heavenly Jerusalem and that, in fact, he was but a stranger and a pilgrim on any earthly soil. Not only Abraham, but all those Old Testament saints, as well, knew that their ultimate goal, their real abiding country was the heavenly land. It was because of this revelation given by God that they had faith to persevere through privations and persecutions as strangers and pilgrims in the present world, bound for the heavenly Jerusalem. These Old Testament saints "all died in faith, (not having received the promise in the heavenly city), but having seen them afar off and were persuaded of them (the certainty of the heavenly life in the New Jerusalem), and confessed that they were strangers and pilgrims on earth." (Heb. 8:11, 13). All these saints knew, therefore, that their promises were heavenly, not earthly. "For they that say such things declare plainly that they seek a country" (not on earth). "They desire a better country, that is a heavenly, wherefore God is not ashamed to be called their God: For He hath prepared for them a city." (Heb. 11:13,14,16). Hence, God prepared a city, the New Jerusalem, for all the saints of Old Testament days.

Jesus himself said that Abraham, Isaac and Jacob were still alive when He verified the words of Scripture spoken by God that "I am the God of Abraham, and the God of Isaac and the God of Jacob. God is not the God of the dead, but of the living." (Matt.22:32). This is to say that God is, not was, the God of these saints. They are living, not dead. God was and is the God of not dead, but of living Abraham, Isaac and Jacob. When the Lord spoke to Moses He said, "I am the God of Abraham", not was. (Luke 20:37,38). When Lazarus died he went to enjoy heavenly blessings with living Abraham. (Luke 16).

Abraham willingly dwelt in tents because he looked for "a city which hath foundations, whose builder and maker is God", where are "the spirits of just men made perfect." (Heb. 12:22,23).

The patriarchs and saints of old from the days of Abel on have gone before to welcome all who have been saved. We, of the New Testament and following times, are the children and grandchildren and succeeding posterity of these saints of old. All "they which be of faith are blessed with faithful Abraham. If ye be Christ's, then are ye Abraham's seed and heirs according to the promise." (Gal. 3:10,29). In other words, saints of later generations, true believers, "they which be of faith", are in a sense spiritual children of Abraham, and of Isaac, and of Jacob, and of the saints who succeeded them Surely we great-grandchildren of the patriarchs do not have heavenly promises and blessings superior to those Old Testament saints. Children do not have precedence over parents. Fortunate are we if we be among them "which be of faith" so that we may be "blessed with faithful Abraham."

New Testament Saints There

Surely there is no time, or race preference, in heaven. It is clearly revealed that the Gentiles are "fellow-heirs" of the same body (as the Old Testament saints), and partakers of His promise in Christ by the Gospel. (Eph. 3:5,6). By special grace we Gentiles of the present church-time are allowed to be "partakers" of the promises, the blessings given the Old Testament saints, and be with them "fellow-heirs" in the city of our God. All the blessings of salvation, and all the promises of eternal life through the Holy Spirit, and the baptism and the fullness of the Holy Spirit, comes through the New Covenant to be made with Israel. We are given just foretastes of the promises that will yet be fulfilled with Israel.

When a pilgrim from earth comes to the city whose builder and maker is God he sees over, or upon, the pearly gates "the names of the twelve tribes of the children of Israel", and upon the "twelve foundations" the "names of the twelve apostles of the Lamb." (Rev. 21:12, 14). He has indeed come to the city of all the saved where is neither Jew, nor Gentile, neither Old, nor New Testament distinctions, or preferences. He has come to the one body, the one family of those born of one Spirit, to the city of all the redeemed who unite around the one throne to sing in unison "the songs of Moses and the Lamb."

This one body of Old and New Testament saints constitutes the one bride of Christ, and that bride is the New Jerusalem. There came unto me one of the seven angels saying, "Come hither, and I will show thee the bride, the Lamb's wife, and he carried me away in the spirit—and showed me that great city, the Holy Jerusalem." (Rev. 21:9,10).

The bride of Christ is the New Jerusalem, the one body of Old and New Testament saints. "Come hither, I will show thee the bride, the Lamb's wife. And he carried me away, and shewed me that great city, the New Jerusalem." (Rev. 21:9,10)

There never was, or never will be, any salvation, but by grace through Christ. By works of the law of God neither Old nor New Testament people could be saved, for all sinned by breaking the law. Though Old Testament saints did not understand the import of the cross, it was not their sacrifices that cleaned them from sin, but their sins were taken from them, so to speak, and stored away to be borne by Jesus, the only sin- bearer. Jesus not only bore the sins of all who trusted God after He came; He also bore all the sins of all who truly trusted God before He came. "He is the mediator of the New Testament (or covenant), that by means of death for the redemption of the transgressions that were under the first testament (old Testament), they which are called might receive the promise of eternal inheritance." (Heb. 9:15).

We see, therefore, that the whole Bible teaches that they who, through faith, trusted God, by His grace became partakers of His divine nature and have gone to His city, "the New Jerusalem."

Some of my friends have been there. They died, left their bodies, took a final look at the body they had discarded, and with the angels ascended to heaven. Those who have been to heaven and returned tell of a wonderful Paradise whose splendors language cannot describe.

That the saints of both the Old and New Testament are now in heaven is also the testimony of the "cloud of witnesses." When caught up to heaven John Bunyan saw and talked with Elijah and other saints, some of present times. Sundar Singh also saw Elijah, Moses and other Old Testament saints and saints of present times. General Booth saw "the patriarchs and apostles of ancient times the holy martyrs—and an army of warriors who had fought in every part of the world and—myriads and myriads of spirits who were never heard of on earth outside of their own neighborhood." Talmage saw departed friends in heaven, "all well, and ruddy, and songful, and abounding with eternal mirth." Another who was permitted to visit the New Jerusalem and sent back to earth to tell about it saw "A multitude which no man could number, amongst whom she recognized patriarchs, and prophets, and apostles, and martyrs, and missionaries who had died in the colony, besides many others whom she mentioned; and, although the parties were not named by the angel that attended her, yet she said that seeing them was to know them."

Without quoting further, suffice it to say that it is the general testimony of those who have been caught up to heaven and come back to tell us about it that in heaven they saw Old and New Testament saints and that they also mingled and talked with their own friends who had died and are now in heaven.

Heavenly Bodies of the Redeemed

The "cloud of witnesses" gives us much clear information about the nature of the bodies of the redeemed Old and New Testament saints now in the heavenly city. When John Bunyan was caught up to the City of God, escorted there by an angel, he was soon led to meet and talk with Elijah. Of this conversation, giving much light on the nature of the bodies of those in heaven, Bunyan wrote:

"'Rather', said I, with some eagerness, 'let me stay here, for there is no need of building tabernacles. The heavenly mansions are here ready fitted.'

"To which my shining messenger replied, 'Here in a while (after death) thou shalt be fixed forever, but the divine will must first be obeyed.'

"Swift as a thought he presently conveyed me through thousands of bright and winged spirits and then presented me to that illustrious saint, the great Elijah, who had lived in the world below so many hundred ages past and gone; and yet me-thought I knew him at first sight.

"'Here's one,' said my conductor, 'who, by the commission from the Imperial Throne has been permitted to survey these realms of light; and I have brought him hither to learn wherein its glory and its happiness consists.'

"'That', said the prophet, 'I will gladly do, for it is our meat and drink in these blessed realms to do the will of God and the Lamb, to sing His praises and serve Him with humblest adoration.' After which he (Elijah) said, 'Now, give attention to what I shall speak. What you have seen and heard already I am sure you never can relate so as to make it understood, for it is beyond what eye hath seen, or ear hath heard, or what the heart of man is able to conceive. Nor is my being here in the body any objection to what I now say: for death, though it has not been subject to the common lot of mortals, death, yet here it suffered such a change as has been in some sense equal thereto (death); for it is made both spiritual and impassible, and is now no more capable of any further suffering than those blessed angels are that compass the throne. And yet, in this full state of happiness, I cannot utter all that I enjoy. Here happiness is always new. I must tell you that when the soul and body both are happy, as mine now are, I count it a complete state of happiness, for through all the innumerable ages of eternity, it is the soul and body joined together in the blessed resurrection state that shall be the continued subject of happiness the divine perfection being infinite, nothing less than eternity admits of new additions; and by a necessary consequence our knowledge of it shall be eternally progressive, too. Sin is the heavy clog of saints while they are embodied in corrupt flesh; and therefore, when they lay their bodies down their souls are like a bird loosed from its cage, and with an heavenly vigor mount up to this blessed region. But here their warfare is at an end, and 'death is swallowed up in victory.' Here their bright souls, that were below deformed and stained by sin, are, by the ever blessed Jesus, presented to the eternal Father without spot or wrinkle. We are freed from the effect of sin and its punishments. We here are all the children of one Father, and all our brethren are alike dear unto us.

Before the time of the resurrection of their bodies the saints of the Lord who have died live in heaven's parks and palaces in spiritual bodies resembling those in the flesh, so that friends recognize and have fellowship with friends.

"'The bodies of the blessed here at the resurrection shall be (as mine now is), spiritual bodies; and by your not only seeing, but touching me (at which word the holy prophet, Elijah, was pleased to give me his hand), you may be the better able to know what I mean by a spiritual body. That is, a body rarefied from all gross alloys and of corruption, and made a pure and a refined body, and yet a substantial body, not composed of mind and air as mortals below are apt too grossly to imagine. 'Have you not read', said the prophet, 'that the blessed Jesus, after His resurrection, appeared in His body to His disciples when they were met together in a chamber and the doors were shut about them? And yet, He called Thomas to come and reach forth his hand and thrust it into His side, which shows it as plainly to be substantial. The vision of our blessed Lord is here (in heaven) what both our souls and bodies live upon and are supported by forever.'

"While I was thus talking, the prophet, a shimmering form, drew near. It was one of the redeemed. He told me that he had left his body below, resting in hope until the resurrection; and that, though he was still a substance, yet he was an immortal one. Here we see not only our Elder Brother Christ, but also our friends and relations. Thus, though Elijah lived in the world below long before your time, you no sooner saw him than you knew him."

Sundar Singh had repeated visions of both Old and New Testament saints in heaven. When in heaven the saints there told him many things about the present heavenly and also the later resurrection state. He says:

"I was told there that Christians leave behind them the physical body. That body is buried, but the spiritual body that is within is then free to come out, and in this (the spiritual body that comes out of the physical) we go to heaven."

In the case of those caught up to heaven without dying, upon inquiry he was told that the physical body "is completely spiritualized, for flesh and blood cannot inherit eternal life; but, it is the same physical body, only completely transformed. I asked then whether this applied to Enoch and Elijah, who were taken bodily into heaven. They told me, 'Yes', and that it also applied to Moses. Then they pointed out to me Moses and Elijah in heaven, and they told me that they appeared at the transfiguration in the same form and aspect in which I saw them then. God buried Moses, but they told me God's way is to enfold in a spiritual body, and this is what happened to the body of Christ."

These far away saints cross the harmless river of death one by one and ascend beyond to the Paradise of God, clothed in spiritual bodies of glory that resemble the mortal bodies their souls inhabited and left at the river's shore.

Another witness tells us: "The angelic being beside me said, 'this body thou seest is the soul, or spiritual body, possessed while in the temple of flesh on earth', and I saw that the form, or outline, of the soul was, and always has been that of the human body." Consequently, between the time of the death of the physical body and the time of the resurrection, the soul and spirit, according to these witnesses, has a spiritual body in appearance like the physical body from which it comes out when the body of clay is discarded.

Those raised from the dead add their sure word of testimony also. Although they knew when they left and when they re-entered their earthly, material body, they also knew they still had a spiritual body. They could see the world about them, and one spoke of feeling the air on her face as she ascended from the earth. It is the testimony of these raised from the dead that, after they were out of the earthly, physical body they still had a real, a spiritual body, in which they could move and talk and enjoy in ways exceeding all that they had been able to do while encumbered by the corrupted fallen body of clay. In reply to my inquiry about the case of Sister Vex, Pastor Gensicthen, who knew the circumstances and who knew and often talked with her, wrote me: "The sister had a great longing to be with the Lord since that experience (having died) through all her following years of life in which she was a blessing to many others." This sister, as well as the little girl of five, who died and came back again from heaven, during the time of her death while "out of the body", still had a body so real that she never again wanted to live in the mortal, earthly body.

After reading the testimonies of those raised from the dead as given in The Three Worlds, a brother in agreement with this wrote me a personal letter, saying: "If you turn to the pages about Mrs. Ward's description of herself and the others you will read what was exactly my own experience. I am now sixty-eight years old and was up in heaven when I was twenty years old. When God sent me back to earth, it was such a pain to me."

The Bible confirms all this, for John "saw under the altar the souls of them that were slain for the Word of God and for the testimony which they held—and white robes were given unto everyone of them." (Rev. 6:9, 11). These saints are clearly said to be the "souls", and it is said that they were everyone of them given "white robes." The Bible, therefore, confirms what heavenly witnesses all affirm that, between death and the resurrection, saints in heaven do have spiritual bodies clothed in white.

No cripples in heaven, every imperfect body discarded by saints on earth, will be succeeded by a perfect spiritual body in heaven.

In view of all these witnesses and the testimony of the sure Word of God, no one need doubt, therefore, that all the Old Testament saints and all the other redeemed men and women who have died from the days of Abel to the present time are now in the heavenly city, the New Jerusalem, with spiritual bodies in which they now enjoy blessing exceeding anything they ever knew on earth.

Attempted Description of Saints

The appearance of those who have died and are free from corruption and imperfection some have tried to describe. All the effect of disease, all the corroding work of age, all the physical blemishes resulting from man's fallen estate are done away in heaven. There is no decrepit person there. General Booth, though attempting to describe persons redeemed from earth as they appear in their glorious spiritual bodies in heaven, at the same time declares that the beauty of saints in heaven beggars description. Of one saint who came to converse with him, he says: "Describe the shape, the features and bearing of this noble form I cannot, and will not attempt it. He was at the same time earthly and celestial. I discovered, therefore, at a glance that he was one of the blood-washed multitude, and I not only judged from a certain majestic appearance which he bore; but, from instinct, I felt that the being before me was a man, a redeemed and glorified man. He looked at me, and I could not help but return his gaze. His eyes compelled me; and in doing so I confessed to being ravished by his beauty. I could never have believed the human face divine could have borne so grave a stamp of dignity and charm; but far beyond the entrancing love lines of those celestial features was the expression through every ligament of that countenance, and through those eyes that were gazing upon me. It was as though that face was only a sun-lit window through which I could see into the depths of the pure benevolent soul within. He spoke first. Had he not done so I could never have summoned courage to address him. His voice was soft and musical and fitted well with the seriousness of his aspect."

General Booth writes of another he met in heaven: "She told me her name. I had heard it on earth. She was a widow who had struggled through great difficulties. After her husband's death she had given herself up unreservedly to fight for the Lord. Her children had been her first care and all but one had been saved.

"There was a dignity of bearing of inward power, the same marvelous expression and purity and joy as in the case of the man just described; but, in this case, combined (I could imagine) with a beauty of more delicate and enthralling mold. Beautiful as I thought my first visitor to be, more beautiful than conception, or dream of earth could be; yet, here was a beauty that surpassed it—not, perhaps, if judged from inherent rules, but judged from my standpoint. My former visitor, I have said, was a glorious man; this was the glorified form of a woman.

"I had, when on earth, sometimes thought I could have wished the privilege of beholding Eve in the hour when she came from the hands of her Maker, and I had imagined something—only something, of what her beautiful form must have been as she sprang into being on that bridal morning, young and pure and beautiful—perhaps the sweetest work of God. Now, here I saw her I saw Eve reproduced before my eyes as young, pure and beautiful, nay, more beautiful than her first mother could possibly have been; for was not this God's finished workmanship?"

This effort to describe how redeemed man and woman appear in their gloried state necessarily fails in completeness, for how can be described to fallen man the glories of the redeemed? The redeemed, resurrected life is higher and more glorious than that of the first Adam and first Eve in the first Eden. The first parents in their perfection beauty were, nevertheless, earthly. The last and heavenly state is spiritual, grandeur and more beautiful than earth ever knew, even in the day of its primitive perfection.

The souls of those who have gone to heaven are clothed with a halo of radiant glory light so bright it would dazzle and blind the eyes of mortal man. This white radiance appears in every conceivable color and hue.

From what great depths to what superb heights has God exalted man! Here was a weak and sinful man from earth, appearing in heaven in such grandeur and beauty that it was hopeless to attempt description. Here was also a poor widow from earth, once occupied with the cares of her bereaved children while gladly devoting her strength to the Lord. Having discarded her earthly body with its encumbrances and cares, escorted by angels to heaven, she lived in a glory in the New Jerusalem that transformed her into a perfected beauty such as Eve had never known in the first perfect Paradise of God.

Saints Clothed With Light

The foregoing description of man and woman in the realms of heaven is but a partial picture as they appeared divested of their halos of glory. Had they appeared in all their auroral glory, General Booth could not have looked upon them, for every person in heaven, like every angel, is surrounded by an aurora of rainbow-light, so brilliant that were it not withheld, no mortal could look upon it. As in the case of the angels, this light seems to emanate from each saint in heaven and the light, having come from the, throne of Christ, carries life as well as light.

This halo, or aurora, varies with the individual and is in accord with the varying degrees of spiritual attainment of the different saints in heaven.

Paradoxical as it may seem, although this halo that surrounds each saint gives the appearance of his being clothed in white at the same time there is the appearance of being clothed in beautiful colors more varied in shades and tints than any of the most colorful sunshine that seems to be but light and yet contains all the prismatic colors of the rainbow. The heaven glory-light, however, far exceeds all this in its inclusive variegated splendors.

Those living in the higher plains, the plains of highest spiritual development and nearest the throne, radiate from their bodies the brightest light. Saints on the lower plains are surrounded by light correspondingly less brilliant. The amount of heavenly aurora-light radiating from each individual saint also varies on each plane, those in more advanced mansions being clothed with more light than others of lower degree.

The light that radiates from the bodies of those who dwell in the highest spheres is so brilliantly resplendent that when they visit the saints who inhabit the lower plains they must to some extent, hide this light under a kind of cloak, so to speak, or those on the lower plains, although themselves spiritual and heavenly, could not look upon those highly advanced saints from higher realms. On the other hand, when saints from lower spheres visit the higher plains they are endued with protecting covering to enable them to stand in their presence and look upon the more advanced saints. This is the testimony of witnesses.

The Scriptures are not silent on this subject of garments of light. When Moses went into the Mount to talk with God face to face, he could not have done so without God's special covering. When Moses returned from his communion in the Mount, his face so shone that the children of Israel could not look upon him. "When Aaron and all the children of Israel saw Moses, behold, the skin of his face shone; and they were afraid to come nigh him. And till Moses had done speaking with them, he put a veil on his face; but, when Moses went in before the Lord to speak with Him, he took the veil off until he came out." (Ex. 34:29-34). If Moses, in his mortal body, could be so clothed upon by heaven's glory-brilliancy after but a short time in the presence of God, what must be the brilliancy of the light that radiates from saints in the highest plains of heaven who dwell for centuries in the light that comes from the throne of God? No wonder that when Moses and Elijah appeared with Jesus on the Mount of Transfiguration (Matt. 17) in their heavenly aurora-light (as saints in heaven told Sundar Singh), Peter and James and John fell upon their faces until Moses and Elijah departed and Jesus again laid aside His heavenly halo.

This light that radiates from heavenly inhabitants, one was told, is the light of the Holy Spirit. This accords with what people often experience when they see the Holy Spirit as light. It also accords with the Scripture which says there are "seven lamps of fire burning before the throne, which are the seven Spirits of God" (the Holy Spirit in sevenfold manifestation). (Rev. 4:5).

The Heavenly Mansions of the Saints

In reading the testimony of the "cloud of witnesses" it is strikingly apparent that the most indescribable of all the marvels of Paradise are the wonderful mansions. Those who have seen them, when returning to tell of their magnificence are utterly at loss for words. They try comparing the mansions of the blessed in heaven with the palaces of the kings of the earth, but their comparison fails. They talk of all the lovely combinations of ivory and marbles and rare woods of earth. They mention decorations of gold and silver with settings of diamonds and pearls and emeralds and every other precious stone known to man, and end by saying that they have miserably failed to picture the gorgeous magnificence of the mansions in the Eden parks of the New Jerusalem. Up there the beautiful stones and woods are much more beautiful and finer in texture and more varied in hue than any on earth. They say that heavenly gems, precious stones, pearls and diamonds are larger than earth has seen and the gems reflect the golden light of the celestial city, emitting radiant shades of delicate colors exceeding the imagination of any mortal.

There are some beautiful homes on our splendid avenues and boulevards on earth which seem grand enough to satisfy any man. Yet our Savior who came down to earth has gone to prepare for His own homes more gorgeous than man has ever built. Though the finest of man's mansions would astonish us, Jesus lavishing His love upon us, has prepared for us better than these.

Bunyan says of the light in the mansions: "All that throughout these heavenly mansions is nothing else but the light that flows with so much transparent brightness emanations of the Divine Glory in comparison of which the light of the sun is but darkness."

Man's first home was in an Eden of paradisiacal wonders, where he walked and talked with God. Man's last home will be in everlasting Eden in jewel-bedecked mansions of paradisiacal beauties far exceeding those at the first perfect Eden. Yes, we shall live with Christ in Paradise.

Angels

The New Jerusalem is a city of angels. "We are come unto the city of the living God, the heavenly Jerusalem. and to the innumerable company of angels", (Heb. 12:22). "to myriads of angels, ten thousand times ten thousand of thousands", (Rev. 5:11). innumerable millions of angels.

In countless numbers angels, singly, or in groups, like glory clouds, fly over every plain in every realm of the holy city, singing praises as they float, or as they poise in the golden glory-atmosphere.

Angels also wander through every park on every plain, and mingle in all the life of heaven's vast domain. There is not a mansion that is not gladdened by the angels' presence, nor is there anyone in all the realms of all the city who does not have the companionship and help of the angels.

In summary, then, we see that the inhabitants of the heavenly city are the redeemed of all men from the beginning of the Old Testament times to the present. The Old Testament saints are in God's city, the New Jerusalem. The New Testament saints are there, too; and so are all later saints who have gone before us in this celestial city in the skies. Here all without distinction, so far as time is concerned, dwell together in the Lord's appointed mansions of light and splendor, all loving members of the family of God in heaven.

These saints in heaven, since they departed from the body of flesh, are living with visible and real spiritual bodies, clothed upon with garments of light and beauty, and their appearance is in such glorious splendor that no language can describe them.

These former inhabitants of earth, now inhabitants of the New Jerusalem in the third heaven, live in the midst of innumerable hosts of God's holy angels who inhabit all parts of the golden city of the redeemed.

THE INHABITANTS OF NEW JERUSALEM

The saints in New Jerusalem!
"The mother of us all", (Gal. 4 :26)
Are all the saved from all the earth
Since day of Adam's fall.

By faith, they're saved by Jesus' blood, I
n His abounding grace:
For only thus the "just" can live
To see Him face to face.

"The law" was not "of faith" at all,
It brought men under "curse:"
To try to find the Lord by works
Made failures worse and worse.

Although not all could see it clear,
The merits of His blood
Was what alone could cleanse from sin—
The cross, the crimson flood.

So now, in jeweled mansions there,
In every place and plain:
The saints are clothed in garments white
And washed from every stain.

Where mortal now immortal is
By spirit clothed upon:
Each, in his proper home and place,
Lives in his Lord alone.

As stars in glory differ, each
Sheds forth the glory-light:
That causes saints on heaven's plains,
Help make all heavens bright.

CHAPTER 7
FROM GLORY TO GLORY

"We all, with open face beholding as in a glass the glory of the Lord, are changed into the same image from glory to glory." (2 Cor. 3:18). The changing of mortal, sinning man, into the final perfection of Christ is a progressive work that be gins on earth and continues in heaven. It is from "glory to glory." While still upon earth a measure of heavenly glory rests upon each saint through the gifts and the endowments of the Holy Spirit. Although this glory differs according to the spiritual development of the individual, it should be in the case of every saint while still on earth a progressive growth.

In heaven the higher glories begin when the earthly restraints are left behind. The saints there, as on earth, differ in bodily glory and spiritual attainment. "There is one glory of the sun, and another glory of the moon, and another of the stars, for one star differeth from another star in glory. So also is the resurrection of the dead." (1 Cor. 15:41,42). True of the state after the resurrection, it is also true of the saints who are in heaven now that they differ in glory. The principle and order in heaven does not change; it is from "glory to glory."

The work of Jesus, begun in the sinner on earth, is to continue after death "from glory to glory" until in heaven he attains to the glory of Christ in the highest sphere. Growth will continue until the saint is developed into the heavenly image and glory of his Redeemer.

Accordingly, all heaven is systematically arranged in one harmonious order as the great "family in heaven", the family of God. From the smallest and weakest babe to the most mature in this family of the redeemed, all under the Father's care, will be cherished and nourished until everyone attains to "a perfect man, unto the measure of the stature of the fullness of Christ." (Eph. 4:13). Though the sins of saints on earth are forgiven and though the saints on earth are washed and made white in the blood of the Lamb, saints on earth nevertheless differ in glory and spiritual attainment and Christ-likeness. Christians differ from the new-born babes in Christ who know little of the life and mystery of salvation, to the mature saints who, through suffering and cross bearing for Christ, have attained to a holy and heavenly walk in Him.

From earth, with its spiritual experiences, it is a progressive step by step upward order through all the successive wards on all the successive plains 'in all of the First and Second, and Third heavens.

While saints are on earth the real heavenly glory, the point to which each has developed in the glory-life of Jesus, is correctly reckoned as the Lord sees values from His viewpoint. His valuation of man's spiritual attainment may differ much from man's estimations. Those who have been leaders in the church on earth may be actuated by such mixtures of selfish motives, not working only for the purpose of getting glory for Jesus, that they hinder the development of their own life in the Spirit of Christ. Judging from their high position of leadership in the work of the Lord on earth men suppose these Christians are far advanced in the glory life of heaven. And yet they may be mere babes in Christ, so that when they enter the land of true values they will need to be taught from the beginning the true worth of the humble Jesus before they can advance to higher spheres and plains. The widow whom General Booth saw in heaven in strength of character and beauty beyond human conception, left her humble sphere of inconspicuous, heart-devoted and self-sacrificing service to her Lord to be promoted to high realms of glory in heaven, while others who on earth seemed mighty to men, were assigned lowest plains of glory and usefulness in heaven.

By God's grace my eyes have been opened to see mountains molded by the hand of the Lord, see trees and flowers by the roadside smiling good will to God and man, and see heaven-sent winged choristers flitting from bough to bough. My traveling companion sees only the path below him. He sees not the glories of heaven in God's handiwork about him.

Herein was the greatest surprise to Talmadge in his vision of heaven. In reply to inquiry as to what impressed him most in heaven, he said: "I was most impressed with the reversal of earthly conditions. I knew, of course, that there would be differences of attire and residence in heaven, for Paul had declared long ago that souls would then differ 'as one star differeth from another', as Mars from Mercury, as Saturn from Jupiter; but, at every step in heaven, I was amazed to see that some who were expected to be high in heaven were low down, and some who were expected to be low down were high up. I found the highest thrones, the brightest coronets, the richest mansions, were occupied by those who had reprobate father, or bad mother, and who inherited twisted natures of ten generations of miscreants, and who had compressed in their body all depraved appetites and all evil propensities; but, they had laid hold of God's alm; they had cried for especial mercy they had conquered seven devils within and seventy devils without, and were washed in the blood of the Lamb. By so much as their conflict was terrific and awful and prolix, their victory was consummate and resplendent; and they have taken places immeasurably higher than those of good parentage, who could hardly help being good, because they had ten generations of piety to help them. The steps by which many have mounted to the highest places in heaven were made out of the cradles of corrupt parentage. I pointed to one of the most colonnaded and grandly domed residences in all the city, and said:

"'Who lives there ?'

"'The widow who gave two mites.'

"Some of those professors of religion who were famous on earth I asked about, but no one could tell me anything about them. Many who had ten talents were living on the back streets of heaven. Infinite capsize of earthly conditions! All social life in heaven graded according to earthly struggle and usefulness as proportioned to use of talents given. Some of the most unknown of earth were most famous in heaven, and many who seemed greatest failures on earth were the greatest successes of heaven." Hence, advancement in the life and spirit of Jesus here on earth determines our state of glory in heaven.

As on earth, so in heaven: the meek, the teachable, the child-like most rapidly ascend "from glory to glory" and quickest reach the highest spheres on the highest plains in the highest heaven where are the throne of God and the throne of the Lamb.

I open my Bible and read, "Seek ye the Lord, all ye meek of the earth. Seek righteousness, seek meekness." (Zep. 2:3). Then I close my Bible and think. "Yes; there are many upon earth who are seeking 'righteousness'; but how many seek the 'meekness?' I feel a fear that few are deliberately and earnestly and sacrificially seeking this jewel which the Lord adjures all on earth to seek. It is down here where we live now, right in the dirt and the filth of the fallen earth that our feet tread every day where we are to seek this heavenly gem, "meekness." Blessed will we be if we find it, for just over the river in that other land the humble will be exalted to walk on highest plains. Meekness is the road of ascent from glory to glory.

These Ka Dos, all baptized at the same time, will not, at death, all arrive in the same mansion in heaven. By the angels they will be assigned to the mansions of spiritual instruction and development best suited to each one, in accordance to his own particular advancement and capacity to appropriate spiritual life when he leaves his mortal body. They differ now. They will differ then. Death will not eliminate all differences.

Visitors from the heavenly land, returning, tell us that the state of spiritual development in which we leave here is the state in which we arrive there. Those who die in low estate of Christian graces will enter plains of lesser glory in the celestial city, while those who walk nearer to God on earth will be escorted to higher plains of glory in God's heaven.

All heaven is arranged to meet the needs of the redeemed and exalt them "from glory to glory." To this end the city of God and all His heavens in His wonderful plan and order, are a series of successive plains and a series of countless heavenly Edens. The mansions, likewise, and other edifices are systematically placed in ascending and perfectly graded arrangement. All heaven is arranged from glory to glory. All these heavenly things being in ascending glory are perfectly adapted to developing the redeemed of earth from glory to glory.

Saints dying on earth are escorted by angels to the heavenly realms. There each saint is welcomed into the mansion, or place of residence, according to his spiritual development on earth and his other moral, intellectual and spiritual conditions. People of like development and needs, upon first entering heaven, dwell in the same part of the city. Kindred spirits dwell together in parks and mansions best suited to their highest enjoyment and former development.

My wife likes to surround her door with flowers and a clean court. My neighboring Ka Do's wife likes to surround her door with cows and pigs. Both love the Lord, but there is a big difference in capacity for appreciation of the works of God in the present world, and there will be a difference in the world to come. But all will develop from glory to glory until capacity for full appreciation will be reached in the case of every child of God — even the most ignorant and undeveloped on earth.

It is impossible for me to give the Ka Dos any idea of the beauty of golden streets and paradisiacal mansions of precious stones and embellishments. To take one of these people out of this village and suddenly put him into a mansion would be painful to him. He would have to make the adjustment gradually. It is the same principle in heaven. There must be gradual adjustment and development. This is scriptural.

Although Jesus is in all heaven and His life and presence is enjoyed by every saint and angel, not all have equal capacity to partake of this glory life. Because of this limited capacity it is impossible for a saint just from earth at once to enter into the fullness of all the exceeding glories of heaven. Christ Himself and all the glories of the celestial city of light are revealed to each one in limited splendor up to the full capacity of each one's appreciation.

Hence, because saints from earth, upon first entering heaven, can appropriate but a limited amount of the heaven life, and because they cannot at first stand in the presence of the glory of heaven's highest plains, and because saints on earth have not attained to the highest spiritual development, they must, upon entering heaven, first live on lower plains of glory. There they are instructed and developed in the heavenly life to be advanced to higher mansions and realms of spiritual instruction as rapidly as their spiritual and intellectual progress will allow.

It appears that few walk so close to Christ in selfless, worldliness, full-hearted devotion to God and in such constant communion with Him in the Holy Spirit that when they die they are directly led to mansions highest up in the holy city. It seems that the choice spirits who enter highest plains of the city at once are a very limited number. This high exaltation immediately upon entering the world of glory belongs, we may well believe, only to earth's rarest saints. Perhaps only such directly enter such realms in the New Jerusalem at death as the Apostle John who rested so near to Jesus' heart, and Mary, who sat at Jesus' feet and lived on His Words of Life, and Saint Francis, and brother Lawrence, and Sundar Singh, and others who daily walk and talk with Jesus and have learned to bear the cross He bore. But those who have not so attained "from glory to glory" on earth must, in God's plan, be led from "glory to glory" in heaven.

This is not because God is any respecter of persons or partial in His love. The gates of loftiest realms in highest heaven are open to all who can attain to enter in.

Neither will any saint from earth be jealous of those in heaven he finds on higher plains than himself. Into what ever mansion in whatever Eden-park the angel guides his pilgrim from earth, the new arrival will find himself in glories so overwhelmingly dazzling that in every way he will find his capacity for enjoyment too limited. He could hold no more. In every way his cup will overflow.

Schools of instruction are on every paradisiacal plain in varying degrees of magnificence, each surrounded by its own particular Eden.

Only as he becomes accustomed to the light and life and inexpressibly intoxicating glories of the mansion and park in which his guardian angel wisely and rightly placed him, and as his capacity becomes enlarged can he advance to more exceeding glories of higher mansions and plains. Nor would he sooner go up higher if he might. The place he is in, the fellowship of those in the part of heaven where he dwells, the spiritual instruction there given are exactly what satisfies and suits him best. He is as happy as any flower growing in a soil and environment exactly suited to its nature, and not envious of any other flower in any other place.

Visiting Shanghai, after many years far away from civilization in the mountains, I was at first dazzled and confused by its beauty, its variegated neon lights, its nicely dressed hurrying peoples of many lands and races. It took me a time to get adjusted. It will be so in heaven. We will get adjusted to increasing harmonies from glory to glory.

I can illustrate the truth of enlarging capacity. After I had for some years lived and worked among mountain tribal people, entirely away from the embellishments of modern life, I found it necessary to visit Shanghai. When I left home and arrived at the first Chinese town with one short street of shops in which were displays of pretty things and I saw cleanly-dressed, bright, wide-awake people crowding the street, I felt ill at ease. By the next morning I was adjusted to the new environment. From there I continued my journey to the capital city of the province. Upon entering this city with its wider streets, its more brilliant shop displays, its better-dressed and keener-minded people, its many rickshas and an occasional automobile, I was confused for days. My mind was too excited to contain its usual composure. It seemed to me that I had come out of darkness into light, out of earth into heaven. When finally I got to Shanghai I was helplessly amazed. So, in heaven it will be amazing for the new arrivals from earth. It will be strange at first and hard to endure the fullest glories. While most saints at death first go to second heaven, the most spiritual may be delayed there but a day or so.

As already stated, while the regular residence of those who enter heaven is in differing degrees of glory in different plains and mansions differing in splendor, on each plain, in God's economy, there is provision whereby saints have access to higher and lower plains than the one where they usually live.

The order "from glory to glory" as revealed is apparently something as follows: Persons like the thief on the cross, and deathbed repentance saints and those who had little experience in the Christian life, and those who never suffered for Christ, or developed spiritual life, are at death ushered into the more remote places of instruction on the lowest, or at any rate one of the lower plains of heaven. Great numbers of mansions and temples of instruction are arranged in ascending grades, the highest rank on each plain being the central edifice on that particular plain, as already stated.

Our beautiful residence avenues in our man-made little Paradise vary in architectural magnificence and in floral and artistic surroundings. No two mansions, no two avenues the same. In heaven, too, is endless variety exceeding the conceptions of man.

While all these mansions of the redeemed are arranged from glory to glory, and the saints are assigned as suited to the mansions, there is not a mansion that does not exceed in grandeur the highest conception of man.

Since all heaven is a spiritual realm, everything in it is spiritual and has spiritual values. The parks of beauty that surround each edifice, the animals, the trees, the flowers, the lakes, the rivers, the crystal pools, the shape and size of the mansions, the gems, the jewels and everything connected therewith: the angels that attend, the angels that instruct, the music, the songs, the saints mingling in fellowship, the degree of manifestation of glory-light and life—all these and everything else in each separate park or palace are harmonious parts. These all contribute to the spiritual life and development of every saint who dwells therein. There is not a flower, or a tree, or a bird, or a stone in a building that does not in some way contribute to the spiritual up- building of the life of the saints, or does not help enlarge their capacities for a more exalted life.

In writing of this Sundar Singh says: "When in this world we see mountains, trees and flowers, we see and admire. In that world also we see and admire objects of the same sort, only there is a kind of force comes from them which gives one an impulse to praise the Creator of it all, and that without any kind of effort, but simply as a spontaneous expression of fullness of joy."

Thus it is that all heaven, all its parks, all its mansions, all its fauna, all its flora, all its lakes, brooks and rivers, and all of the life of saints and angels in all relationships are one harmonious, progressive, inter-related, whole, arranged and advancing "from glory to glory."

In short, then, we see that all is "from glory to glory", from lowest park and plain and mansion, but all is "glory", the glory that is celestial and glory upon glory, "from glory to glory" until the weakest saint will sometime, through the ages, stand in highest spheres on highest plains in highest heaven. He will have attained "from glory to glory" to the measure of the stature of the fullness of Christ. He will have attained to His perfect image who sits on the throne. 52

Each paradisiacal home in heaven has its own grandeur in design, its own surrounding in edenic beauties differing in detail. The arrangement is "from glory to glory." Mansions are "from glory to glory." Streets are "from glory to glory." The innumerable plains in the heavens are "from glory to glory." All is "from glory to glory", and yet, all is in exceeding glory.

As love covets love, and as love wants reciprocal love, in that glad day of consummation those in the New Jerusalem, the redeemed from the days of Adam and all who shall yet enter the city, will be perfect with the Bridegroom, one in love, filled with all the fullness of God (Eph. 3:19) to live and reign with Him in glory for ages and ages and all eternity.

FROM GLORY TO GLORY

It is glory here, and it's glory there:
And it's glory all of the way,
As we make our journey day by day
From earthly night to the city bright
And the full-orbed life we all will share.

As babes we're born in the family of God:
To grow in His life each day;
While on earthly plain, we still must stay,
In its shadowy night and its dimmer light
To follow the path our Savior trod.

In higher plains in the heavenly land:
In the realms of God above
Where sin is gone and we live in love,
In mansions fair on the plains up there
Are constant calls to higher strand.

In a Paradise on a heaven's plain:
Where angels stroll with harp and song
It's glory to glory all along,
As hearts expand in Jesus' hand
And chords are caught from higher strain.

From mansions bright to those more fair:

From plains below to the plains above,
It's so arranged by the Lord in His love
That, as babes we begin, and progress then,
'Till we stand by the Lord as the Lord's joint heir.

CHAPTER 8
PERFECTED BODY AND BODY-SENSES

The "cloud of witnesses" by divine revelation further teach that:

Man will be perfected in heaven. God made man—a human being—in His likeness, and having breathed His divine Spirit into him, created a mortal to walk with Him, a God- man, through eternity. Satan and sin have distorted all the human part of man and have cut off the divine part from fellowship and life with God. Jesus, coming to earth, partook of man's nature, that through His redeeming work He might rescue him, lift him out of earthly realms and perfect him in the realms of heaven.

The Lord came to save, not only man's soul. He came to save his body as well, came to save the whole man. Accordingly, all that was at first man's inheritance——body, soul and spirit—will at last be redeemed by Christ, perfected in Him and transformed to a higher and more blessed state than that of his primal glory.

Thus, all man's bodily senses and functions, as once planned by God, are parts of redeeming grace through Him who was God and man in one— God-man, Jesus.

During life on earth man's physical senses are distorted, at death they are set free. All of the five .senses of the Christian will, therefore, be projected into the life beyond the grave, free from all encumbrances, to be perfected in heaven.

In old age the physical senses — taste, smell, sight, hearing — become increasingly hampered by the decline of all bodily functions. Heaven will reverse the inroads of age. The old will become young again.

The Perfected Body

Our souls are impaired and our spirits are scarred and enslaved in our degenerated, sin- encumbered mortal bodies. Our physical bodies enslave our souls in earthiness. Although of the earth earthy, the delicate tissues of healthy children, inhabited by souls and spirits fairly free, are the most like the primitive pattern given in the Eden on earth.

Happy children run and frolic, and dance and play. Even their muscles seem to rejoice in the beautiful spring time of life. Their souls and spirits share in childhood's freedom. Joys are exuberant, delights unbounded, loves unfeigned and hopes undimmed. Eyes sparkle, ears hear; minds are impressionable; hearts are open; food is delicious; music is charming; death is far away; heaven is all about.

Increasing age changes all this. Dimmer and dimmer becomes the image of God. Man was made in the image of God, and children more nearly retain the impress of the first pattern. But weakening bodies, subject to disease and death, blur the image more and more. How our bodies of clay hamper the man within! Would we fly like angels on ministries for the Lord, our bodies weight us like stone. Would we work with our hands all that our heart finds to do, our exhausted bodies hold us back. Would we think as clearly all of the time as we do in our best moments, our brain gets foggy and sleepy. We tire when we pray, and we get weary when we sing. The things we would do we do not, and the things we would not do we do. Verily men live in bodies distorted by sin. "Even we, ourselves (Christians) groan within ourselves, waiting for the adoption, the redemption of our bodies." (Rom. 8:23).

Because of this, death is not an awful day for the true Christian. It is the day for which, consciously or unconsciously, he has always groaned, the day of his liberation from the hindering body, the day of his ascent to realms of glorious freedom.

In heaven people are free from all the limitations of the mortal body. Youth is restored with all its exuberance, its joys, its unbounded happiness, its sunshine. The joys of youth are so multiplied that to compare them with the joys of the redeemed in heaven is to fall as far short as earth is below the heavens. On earth children may sometimes dance like the angels, but in heaven we shall all dance in pure joy with the angels and the glorified redeemed.

Youth with all its exuberance, its joys, its unbounded happiness, its sunshine will be more than restored in heaven. Free from imperfect mortal bodies that hinder, in new heavenly bodies all that makes youth happy will be multiplied ten thousand fold. In youth all the physical senses — taste, smell, sight, hearing — are best.

In heaven the young will have their joys increased ten thousand times and all the old will become young again. Upon them will be no mark of sickness or scar of deformity. The infirmity of old age will be done away. All the hindrances of the body will be gone, for a better spiritual body is the heritage of everyone. Our friends over there in the land of the redeemed are "all well and abounding with eternal mirth", says Talmage.

No one will ever again get tired. No one will see a sickness, or feel a checking from an imperfect body. In heaven unwieldy bodies will never hinder service for the King. Where we desire to go, as quick as thought we shall arrive. We can walk in all the parks and dance by crystal rivers, but to go we need not walk. As quick as thought we can go anywhere.

Perfected Taste

Man's sense of taste has lost its primitive perfection. From childhood to old age this sense becomes weaker and weaker. In old age the fruits that were so delicious in youth seem to have lost their flavor. No pies, or cakes, or cookies can be found as fine in flavor as those we ate in our childhood home. As surely as man grows old his sense of delicate flavors vanishes.

In heaven, in this matter as well as in others, youth will more than be restored. It will be glorified to higher perfection than youth upon earth. In the gardens of the paradise-city are all the delicious fruits, good for food, that our earth has ever grown. To these are added countless kinds, surpassing what the first Eden of God ever grew, while plain after plain, in ascending magnificence, adds an ever increasing variation.

When we ascend to the spheres above where there is "eating and drinking in the kingdom of God", we shall be enabled to partake of the endless varieties of heavenly fruits and to appreciate their flavors with a sense of keener taste than that of any earthly "professional taster."

As all the fruits in the gardens of God have spiritual life-giving value, each inhabitant will find himself endued with an enlarged capacity of appreciation for all of heaven's fruits and manna, agree all who have been in Paradise.

Life in heaven, unlike life on earth, need not constantly partake of food to maintain existence. All in heaven have everlasting life in Christ and always live in His life. There is, nevertheless, eating of fruits with their special benefits which bring additional phases of life. Drinking of the living waters also has value for the spiritual growth and enlarged capacities of the citizens in the heavenly kingdom.

Preparation of tasty foods to satisfy our God-given desire for foods is one of our main occupations on earth. In Paradise above we will eat again with greater enjoyment than did Adam and Eve in the Garden of God.

Much of man's effort on earth is spent in the search for food and in its preparation. When the Lord placed perfect man in the perfect Eden he was given "every herb and tree for food." When man fell the curse made it necessary for him to eat his bread by the sweat of his brow.

Much of man's earthly enjoyment consists in eating delicious foods. Though largely thwarted by the entrance of sin, these God-given enjoyments of our first parents will be more than realized in eating the heavenly food. Man will partake of heaven's varied fruits with a more refined sense of appreciation than any he has enjoyed on earth.

Fruits that seem to have lost flavor as we grow old, will again be eaten with more delightful enjoyment than ever our youth experienced. The supernatural taste for heaven's delicacies will be one of our surprises.

Perfected Olfactory Sense

In heaven the sense of smell is so refined by the perfected order of life that it can detect a thousand perfumes that earth has never known. If the thousand kinds of roses, the jasmines, the honeysuckles, the carnations, the violets, the tuberoses, the lilies, the lily of the valleys, the lilacs, the magnolias and all the blossoms of fragrant trees and shrubs on earth could be multiplied to grow in profusion in every plain, nook and dell, all this fragrance would be but a hint of the perfumes emanating from the flowers in heaven's paradisiacal parks. All flowers and perfumes earth has ever known, plus untold new varieties are in heaven's Paradises. Those, made new in Christ, who walk the city of the King, are given a perfected sense of smell that enables them to appreciate all these perfumes that pervade the air. If a man on earth, as is said in current news, can distinguish the aromas of a thousand perfumes, what must perfection in heaven mean? In heaven this sense will be enlarged beyond all earthly comparison and will develop in increasing enjoyment from sphere to sphere.

The perfumes of hyacinth, and lilies, and roses, and carnations, and all the perfumes of earth's sweetest floral extracts are but occasional breezes from higher plains that waft to this storm-tossed earth a few of heaven's aromas. In heaven alone will we have capacity to appreciate the ten thousand perfumes that, as distilled sweetness from Eden's flowers, fill the whole atmosphere of Paradise.

Perfected Hearing

Like people we read about, we "have ears and hear not." The music of heaven is all about us, and we catch not its melody. Heaven-sent feathered choristers carol all along the way, while untrained ears catch not the strain. A thousand visitors stroll through a park resonant with the songs of birds, yet scarcely one of them hears a note. In their search for daily bread a million people march by rippling brooks and never hear a murmur. In the falling shades of night the cricket chirps and the whip-poor-will calls from the woods, but farmers, unheeding, after the tiresome work of a sultry day, have ears only for the price of grain and the deadening sound of dollars and cents.

As they play children sing simple songs in heavenly sweet voices, and their elders, with deafened ears, hear only "a noise." What is harmony, and what is discord the disrupted ear cannot discern. Jazz and jingle muddle many, while the din and roar and clang of metallic reverberations from a material world have made its millions deaf. Jumbled notes and chords galore and songs without a soul confuse the ear and spoil the sense that might have enabled it to hear the songs the angels sing.

At best, the songs of the birds we want to hear, the voice of the good we want to heed, the music of the best to which we love to listen, we imperfectly hear and appreciate only in part. Our hardened ears cannot distinguish the finer strains of the first heaven that sings about us.

It is not that way where Jesus is. It is not that way where He has prepared His mansions for those who live in the city far above the clashing sounds of the Satan-disrupted chaotic earth. All heaven is music, morning, noon and night (but "there is no night there.") Every ear is tuned to hear the heavenly harmonies. There is not a sound in all the realm of heaven unlike harmonic music, nor is there an ear which cannot hear it. With earthly cumbrances discarded and ears made anew all rejoice to hear the heavenly symphonies of saints and angels.

Songs sweeter than the mocking birds' and the nightingales' fill with carols of praise the spring-like air of every park. From the flowering fruit trees by every mansion-door the birds light upon the shoulders of those passing beneath the verdant boughs to join the saints in mutual praise. They let the children pet and stroke them and sing with them the children's songs to Him who made and loves and feeds them all. Not God alone, but everyone there is able to hear the songs the children and the cherubs sing as well as all the songs of birds and saints and angels that makes every park in heaven ring.

As has been said, all heaven is an unbroken, perfect harmony. In park, or home, or plain, everything moves in rhythm, the rhythm in which the stars and suns go moving and swinging and singing.

In heaven all ears, tuned in with God, hear music in all its life in strains so celestial that no earthly ear could hear the chord. Those who have listened to the choirs of multitudes of the redeemed have tried in vain to reproduce the hymns of praise they heard. The human voice is too coarse, heavenly music reaches heights and entrancing shades of refined sweetness that none but the spiritual ears of saints in heaven could hear.

We may be so deafened by the world's struggles or inharmonious clanging that our ears fail to catch the murmur of the brook, or hear the singing of the birds among the branches above it. It will not be so where rivers of living waters flow and ears are tuned to hear all of heaven's music.

Much of this soul-satisfying music is all about us in our first heaven, but our ears are too deaf to hear it. In the heavens above the lost chords will all be restored, and the retuned ears from earth will hear again the perfect strains from golden harps.

But, even so, the place our ears begin to really hear is down here on this present earth. Here it is that our ears first learn to listen to words from heaven above, and our souls begin to hear the songs the angels sing.

When reaching realms of glory, everyone will be guided to park, or jeweled mansion, to listen to and join in everlasting songs of praise. Then as the heavenly ear becomes trained to listen to this finer music of loftier praise, the redeemed will be led to higher seats in heaven's choir.

In heaven the highest joy is to give worship and praise and service unto Him who loved us and bought us with His blood, unto Him who is our all in all. Thus the harmonies the heavenly ear is tuned to hear, and the heavenly chords that are played on the heartstrings of each one, and the songs that are sung until they resound in every soul, will all be repeated by all who learn to hear.

Perfected Sight

The depths of the soul reach expression in music. In all heaven there is not a person who will not learn to sing in anthems divine all that is in his love-filled heart. In Paradise, eyes will be clarified to see all the loveliness in all the beauties of Gloryland.

"Lord, that I might receive my sight", was the one yearning heart-appeal of the blind man. On earth, how little we see! How blind we are! True, we live in a world of darkness, but still we are so blind that in broad daylight we see but little. At best we see men as trees, walking.

In heaven there is no impaired eyesight, no blurred, or distorted image. Youthful vision, restored, is multiplied a hundredfold. One caught up to heaven thought he could see a million miles. Another was amazed to find that he could see, through vast distance, people and objects that, on earth, would require a strong telescope. In God's country vision has limitless range.

On earth mental blindness affects one's eyes. Passing by thousands of flowers, we see not a petal. Beautiful birds with brilliant plumage flit before our eyes, and not one attracts our notice. We walk through pastures green where snowy flocks are feeding without seeing a lamb. Children joyfully romp about us unnoticed, and a hundred beauties that we are too blind to see daily pass our door.

We are too blind to see the hand before our eyes. If we endeavor to draw the face of a watch at which we have looked a dozen times a day for twenty years, we find we cannot do it correctly. Though we looked at the watch, we never once really saw it. The average reader can read a page in which are fifty misspelled words and notice scarcely an error.

Blind as we are to the everyday things always before our eyes, we are blinder yet to the great pictures which God has spread before us. Whole mountains of scenic beauty fail to attract our attention from the path upon which we intently fix our homeward gaze. Valleys with rippling rills and wide plains carpeted with daisies, suffice not to excite so much as one admiring glance. God's canopy of sparkling stars hangs over us, and heaven is all around us; yet, we see it not. Upon the earth we grope about with dimmed and daily failing eyesight—the blind leading the blind.

In all these things children have a better sight. They notice all that is about them. That which passes before their eyes they see—at least see more clearly. What moves about them attracts their attention; but, living in the fallen world, with the curse of age and death upon us, the powers of darkness make us blinder day by day until the time of our liberation. And what a liberation that day will be the day we leave this crippled body of befogged and failing sight and ascend from this smoky, eye-blinding earth.

Children's eyes are keenest to see all that is about them. The older we become the less we see. Every soul that enters any plain of heaven will say, "Now, at last, I have arrived at home, sweet home. My soul rests here."

As we enter Paradise, even its lowest plains of glory, our earth-weakened eyes must be shaded to enable us to look steadily on the least of God's celestial wonders. Every arrival in Paradise will declare with astonishment: "Whereas I was blind, now I see." He will realize that he never before saw the hidden beauty in a lily. He never before knew what the Lord meant when He said, "Consider the lilies of the field—I say unto you that even Solomon, in all his glory, was not arrayed like one of these." (Matt. 6:28,29). In heaven he will know that on earth he never did consider the lily for his eyes were too blind to see its beauty.

In Paradise every flower will be a marvel, every petal will be admired. The beauty of every feathered songster will be appreciated by all who move through heaven's parks. Clarified eyes will be open to all of Eden's beauty. Not a fern, or a palm, or a moving branch will escape the notice of eyes that God has enabled to sparkle with delight at the beauties to be seen in all the works of His creation. Whereas on earth we have eyes that see not, in the land of perfection we shall have eyes that never miss a mark of God's unending splendors.

From glory to glory, from plain to plain and from palace to palace our gladdened eyes will never cease to behold new wonders and elicit praise for every beauty the Savior of men has prepared for those who love Him. All of these glories regarding men's perfected senses, and more, are truths of heaven's realities that visitors from there would impress upon us.

PERFECTED MAN

Perfect body, perfect mind,
Perfect heart that's always kind;
Perfect love in all its ways,
To last throughout eternal days.

Perfect ear to always hear,
Perfect music, far and near;
Perfect eye to always see
Eden's beauties that shall be.

Perfect taste and touch and all,
Perfected from curse and fall;
Perfect thought to always know
When to stay and when to go.

Perfect harmony in life,
Perfect spirit—never strife;
Perfect calm, eternal peace
Where perfections never cease.

Perfected by Jesus' grace,
From all limits time and space,
Quick as thought to go, or come
Through the universe—our home.

Perfect beauty—nothing more,
To make each saint each one adore;
A united perfect whole—
Body, spirit and the soul.

Perfect man in Eden there,
Is such that those who saw declare:
That not a mortal ever can
Describe a heaven's perfect man.

CHAPTER 9
PERFECTED SOUL AND SPIRIT

Perfected soul rest! At home at last is the feeling of every soul that arrives in heaven. The restless soul rests. The soul, after its uneasy sojourn on earth, is quiet at last. The soul that was never satisfied is at peace. The redeemed say, "Now my soul has found its home. Here is the place it has always sought. No longer will it be disquieted with in me. Never again will I seek soul-rest. I have come to my Utopia. This is my home, sweet home, where my soul shall never hunger, or wander, any more. I have entered the haven of rest; I will sail the wide seas no more. My soul that was disjointed has slipped into place. I am come to my Father's house. I sit among harmonious brothers and sisters. I find myself resting in perfect peace, in complete satisfaction, entirely happy, overflowing with ecstatic joy." Everyone who reaches a home in any realm of heaven will know at once that he has attained the consummation of every holy aspiration.

Perfected Mind

On earth we have seasons, or days, or hours, or momentary flashes when our minds seem unusually clear, as if clouds had rolled away and the smoky atmosphere had be come clear in a noonday sun. We have times also when special anointings of the Holy Spirit clarify our minds; we think clearly as if we were led to a mountain peak and enabled to see unusual distances through a transparent atmosphere.

These flashes of clear thinking are foretastes of heaven. Over there, where the air is as "lovely as June and invigorating as October" every mind on the celestial plains is clear. The renewed and illuminated brain can think rapidly, clearly and accurately. The intellectual faculties are so quickened that in a few moments it is possible to think through problems that would take years on earth, our witnesses declare.

No faulty memory, no confusion of thought, no imperfections of mind ever falls to the lot of any of God's people in the realms above. Clear thinking, right thinking, deep thinking, divine thinking, is the heritage of all who dwell in heaven. And thus, from school to school, from plain to plain, from realm to realm will the mind be enlarged day by day, year by year, age by age, world by world, worlds without end.

Perfected Knowledge

On earth the wisest know but little, and at our best we "see through a glass darkly." Not so in heaven. Although increasing knowledge will continue throughout the ages, upon entering the heavenly realm we shall marvel at the revelation of truth and knowledge in their true relation and clear understanding. As Talmage says "My walk through the city explained a thousand things that on earth had been to me inexplicable." Other heavenly visitors also noted this wonderful enlargement of knowledge and ability to see things in their right relationships that had on earth seemed to be contradictory, or unexplainable mysteries. Many of the truths of the Bible that puzzle us, truths over which the church on earth divides and splits into antagonistic sects, will be seen in proper relationship and light.

Since Paul, in spite of all his revelations from the Lord, wrote, "Now we see through a glass darkly", surely the rest of us should believe that now we, too, "see through a glass darkly." We should not be too dogmatic about the truths we seem to see so clearly. Although we may be convinced that we are right, do we not need to remind ourselves that we may not see all truth in its proper proportions and relationships? Our selfish interests are so deep-seated, our preconceived ideas so entrenched, personal prejudice so over whelming, and our degenerated reasoning powers so erroneous, that with Paul the most sincere seeker after truth can honestly, if he knows himself, say: "I see through a glass darkly. I know little. I am but picking up pebbles of truth by the great ocean of undiscovered truth. What truth I do know I am unable to fit perfectly into its proper place in its right proportion and emphasis with all other truths."

Yet the main highway to the city of God is made so clear that no one need make a mistake. At the cross-roads of life the Lord has His guide-posts act in the Word of God in letters so large that the way-faring man need not miss his way to heaven, or wander uselessly over the earth. However, should we not humbly admit that in our fallen, unsaved estate we have missed much of the truth? Though born again of the Holy Spirit, in our regenerated state we are still, while on earth, catching but here and there a glimpse of reality. We see rays of sunlight shining through a forest of hindrances. Would not a humble admission of our partial knowledge make us more Paul-like and enable us to work more lovingly with our fellow-pilgrims? Too often we thoughtlessly and ignorantly jostle one another on the King's highway toward the land of truth where we must at last unitedly worship Him who is the Truth.

"Now we see through a glass darkly; but then face to face: now I know in part; but then shall I know even as I am known." (1 Cor. 13:12). "Then we shall know." Then we shall see truth face to face. Then we shall be free from all error. We shall be filled with true knowledge to the full capacity of our renewed minds to comprehend. Then all the knowledge we have already acquired we shall recognize as being but a drop of God's eternal ocean of truths whose depths eternity alone can fathom. What knowledge we then shall have we will hold in humble love. We shall be meekly open to increasing knowledge imparted to us by saints and angels from realms above. In turn we will humbly impart the truth we already possess to those ascending from plains below us.

While on earth in our best regenerated estate we know but little. We see but rays of truth shining through a forest of unexplored realities.

Perfected Intuition

Although there is no sense named "the sixth sense", we may so term this faculty of describing a heavenly blessing little known on earth. This is a perfection of the life of heaven whereby truth is known in some such way as upon earth we speak of knowledge by "intuition." Intuition is a slight foretaste of a fuller fruition in the life to come.

The honey bee knows, without being taught, how to build with the least wax a cell that will hold the largest possible amount of honey. This hexagonal cell is of such perfect geometrical measurements that men could not improve the plan and yet the bees, untaught, working in unison and perfect co-operation, build this perfect cell in the dark. This is knowledge without instruction. This is perfect co-operation when a whole swarm of bees do intricate work that puzzles the minds of men, and they do it all in the dark without any language. With this same perfection and in much the same way, perhaps in exactly the same way, God's whole family in heaven, from the lowest plain to the highest, all work together. Each member does his particular work. An unseen power from the throne co-ordinates everything—intellectual, and emotional, and spiritual elements within each individual—so that all co-operate perfectly in one great plan.

There is language in heaven that all can speak and understand without being taught; but, there is also knowledge without its being consciously acquired. Like the bees in the swarm, each one fits into the plans of all, each knows the thoughts of all, each cooperates with all "intuitively" or by means of this mysterious knowledge that all possess, an enlightenment of the Holy Spirit.

Each person knows what the other thinks before he speaks. By this heavenly intuition, though our friends who have preceded us to heaven have been greatly changed, we will recognize them every one. Although children may have developed into youth, or middle age, and although the old and decrepit will have changed to vigorous middle age, the earthly being discarded, they will appear in glorious spiritual bodies, and we shall know them all. We shall not be disappointed by their change; but consider it a manifold improvement over the form and appearance in which they left us on earth. Without being told, our friends will know when we arrive in heaven and they will come to welcome us in park or mansion.

It will also be known to us which saints are in heaven as the result of our work on earth. We may never have seen many of them; but, by some act, or result of our money, they may have been led to Christ, though we were unaware of it. However, we shall know them all in heaven, and they will know that they are there because we led them there. We shall know this without being told, and together we shall meet and rejoice in praising the Lamb for sinners slain, who loved and saved us all.

In like manner, without introduction, we shall know the patriarchs and saints in heaven. Abraham, Daniel, Moses, the prophets and the apostles we shall know as soon as we see them, and we shall see every one of them. There is, then, in heaven a higher knowledge than man now possesses, or if he does possess it, it is only in a small degree. This heavenly knowledge is known without being taught and is intercommunicated without language.

Scientists know that this "intuitive" sense we call instinct is found in all the natural creation in humanly unexplainable measure.

The homing pigeon inerrantly flies to its home. Year after year the robin returns at the right season to build its nest in the old apple tree. The oriole weaves its hanging nest, and the nuthatch knows how to find its food beneath the bark and where to raise its young in the hollow of the tree. Insect, and worm, and bird, and beast all know where and how to find the proper food and how to avoid an enemy. The humming birds work in pairs building their minute nests. Ants and bees work in colonies, or swarms, in perfect co-operation building geometrically perfect homes and they co-operate in caring for their young, and in doing their own perfect little bit in life without being taught, without a language or a visible way of communicating thought. They do not think; they do not reason; yet they know.

All this is but an imperfect illustration of God's great colony, or swarm, "more than any man can number", in the countless plains within and without His everlasting city, where His knowledge, now working in all the silent creation, will reach harmonious perfection in every bird, beast and man.

Every living creature in heaven possesses this intuitive knowledge, according to his capacity and position in God's economy. In redeemed man this intuition increases as development enlarges the capacity and the need for it. This, like all other blessings in redemption, is "from glory to glory", as the redeemed rise to higher heights in the spheres of pure unbounded knowledge of the mysteries of God.

Perfected Spirit

The voice of every saint is music. The words that fall from the lips of a saint are like drops of honey-dew. Every look is a love look. Not an unspoken word, not a hidden thought, not a reservation. Love flows like a river where everyone is pure, and everyone is in love with everyone else. No one in heaven can refrain from loving others, who are so beautiful and gracious. A perfect spirit pervades all heaven.

As spoken words are like songs of love, so is every action a gracious movement of harmonic rhythm. All the awkwardness, all the clumsiness of physical bodies is gone. Every step, every motion of the hand, every movement of the body is in tune with the music the angels sing. The body, the face, the voice, the affections, though in different degrees, are all tuned in with Jesus, so that one spirit in heaven makes a great [perfected harmony].

Perfected Harmony

All are parts of one harmonic whole. In all heaven there is not a discord, not a rasping voice, not an unrhythmic motion, not an ill-spoken word, and not an unkind thought. Although the multitude in heaven is more than any man can number, and all have been discordant inhabitants of an inharmonic earth, in heaven each one retains his earthly identity. Purified in the waters of eternal life, he becomes a part of heaven's perfect symphony. In all that vast symphony there is not a note out of harmony, nor an instrument out of tune.

There is harmony in thought: not a selfish thought can be found within the jasper walls. Light from the Throne of Christ so shines into every heart that all thoughts are as clear as though visible. No concealment there, no hidden motives, no unholy purposes. Because all love Jesus supremely, all love one another.

There is not a dislikable flaw in any saint in heaven. Perfect love in all of God's perfected people makes all Paradise a paradise of love.

Perfected Love

Love of Jesus, pure and free from all that is physical, material, sexual, gross and unrefined, fills every heart in heaven with a similar love. As Jesus loves every saint, so does every saint love every other saint. Love, pure and undefiled, between the saints in heaven is more beautiful and thrilling than ever was love between friend and friend, man and man, woman and woman, or man and woman, even when that love was pure and accompanied with the blessing of the Lord's Holy Spirit. How can we poor, depraved mortals on earth comprehend this surpassingly incomprehensible love between saints in heaven? This love in itself makes all heaven a paradise.

I remember a Christian bachelor of fifty. He fell in love with a fine Christian girl. All his friends noticed a transformation in every aspect of his demeanor. He dressed neater he walked differently; in his contact with people he talked differently. Most striking of all, he looked different. His face took on such a new expression that time seemed to have turned him back to youth. He seemed to have become another man.

The pure, refined love between all in heaven exceeds all this. Deeper, sweeter, and more ravishing than purest love between lovers on earth is the love of Jesus which fills every heart with waves of holy love that knows no bounds. This love will never grow cold. Here is love in its highest and purest form, a love that will stand the test of time, a love that will grow between soul and soul through days and months and years and ages, and through eternity.

No one in heaven will ever tire of another. All that mars the best in man is done away in heaven. The veil that covers the beauty in each soul is taken away. The made over man and the made-over woman and the made-over son or daughter in heaven are made over with all that is unlovely left out, and all that is lovable, admirable and beautiful retained, retouched and refined. Every person bathes in the river of the water of life until all that is worldly is washed away. All that irritates and detracts disappears. Love and beauty alone remain. All are pure, all are perfect, all are in love with everybody else in heaven. All is love.

Perfected in Jesus' Love

Every physical and spiritual hindrance to the inflow of the love of Jesus being removed, the influent life of Jesus is beyond any earthly Christian experience, even at times of the baptism and fullest anointing of the Holy Spirit. The Lord, at times, has poured out His Holy Spirit in such over whelming floods of love and glory that men, while still in mortal bodies, have felt constrained to ask Him to stay His hand. They could not contain such floods of love-life. And yet all this is but a mere foretaste of the inflow of the love-life of Jesus that fills to overflowing the spiritual capacity of every person in the city of God. At all times and in every place in heaven, even when not in the visible presence of Jesus, the redeemed receive this inflow of love life from Jesus. To those in His presence every ray of glory light, radiating from the body and face of Jesus, carries waves of quickening love. Every glance from Jesus' eyes brings thrills of love; every smile expresses love; every word from His lips carries new discoveries of love that give greater capacities to love in turn. Hence, this enlarged appreciation of the love of Jesus, and the unhindered ability to return to Him spirit-inspired praise, love, worship and service are the supremely outstanding blessings of all the sons of the Redeemer.

Perfected God-Man. One With Jesus

The supreme joy of every person in heaven is the spiritual joy of being one with Jesus. To be filled fully with His life and love, with the body, soul and spirit wholly endued and overflowing with the light and life of the resurrection is to be one with Jesus. The glory that flows from the throne, filling all heaven and every being with light and life, glorifies everything there. The life of Jesus, the life in the Holy Spirit, perfects the reborn in every aspect of life and enables him to appreciate and enjoy the unfathomable blessings of the celestial city. Just as all the blessing of heaven and the life of the redeemed combine to make one harmonic whole, so also in each one who is a part of His life is but a harmonious part of the one harmonic whole—body, soul and spirit.

The redeemed, transformed from glory to glory, will at last become one with Christ in His full stature and in His full likeness body, soul and spirit—Jesus' final work of redeeming grace, man and God in one. Then will every redeemed man become a perfect God-Man: one in Christ, one with Christ, one like Christ—the God-Man, the Bridegroom and the Bride, not TWO—ONE, a multitude of individuals no man can number, yet ONE—MAN MADE DIVINE.

WE WILL MEET AGAIN

When we parted at the river,
And they crossed to yonder shore:
While our hearts ached at the breaking
Of the ties we'd had before,
Angels came from glory-mansions,
Waving palms in heaven's light:
Came to comfort, soothe and cheer us,
Till the dawn should follow night.

Onward went the ones who left us,
As they followed angel guide:
Into Paradise's wonders
To the place they would abide.
In the jeweled mansions' splendors,
In the land of perfect love:
Where their dear ones came to meet them,
Who for long had dwelt above.

Though they went beyond our eyesight

As we gazed across the strand,
Through the tears unbidden, falling,
Since we could not understand
Why they had so early left us,
Hastening through the golden gate:
We will surely e're long join them
In the glory, where they wait.
'Tis a better land than this one

On that fairer, brighter shore,
Where we'll join in that reunion—
Praising God forever more.

HEAVEN'S HARMONY

The life of Jesus, everywhere
In parks and mansions, fills the air,
So every word and every step
Is to the music that is kept
In joyful chords within the heart
Of all who up there have a part.

The birds all sing concordant praise
In music of a thousand lays,
As though each were a separate part
That shares the pulses from one heart:
That leads them as a perfect choir,
To sing His praises, hour by hour.

The ferns and flowers, and palms and trees,
Are swayed in rhythm in the breeze
That, like the scented breath of God,
Is wafted everywhere abroad.

Beneath the boughs that rhythmic sway,
The children dance and run and play;
And tripping like the angels' tread,
Go skipping where the flowers spread
A carpet made of every hue,
By crystal streams where all is new.

And there are times in heaven's days,
When, from within, there rises praise
That causes all that's in that land—
A multitude that's as the sand,
In one united song to sing
The wonders of their Lord and King.

CHAPTER 10
ANGELS SERVING IN HEAVEN

Every angel and saint in all high heaven share the spirit of Him, "who, being in the form of God—took upon Him the form of a servant." (Phil. 2 :6, 7). To humbly and wholly serve Him "who made himself of no reputation" is the most cherished hope of all in heaven. Angels serve Him and worship before Him, laying their crowns at His feet to crown Him Lord of all.

While the fullness of angelic ministry in heaven is far beyond comprehension, even were it revealed, the main out lines of part of this ministry are made known for our encouragement. The heavenly ministry of angels harmoniously fits into the varying degrees of service in the plains of glory that have been mentioned. As angels differ in power, differ in glory, and differ in radiant appearance, so do they also differ in service. There are angels of highest rank—Michael, the archangel (Jude 9) and Gabriel, who stands in the presence of God (Dan. 9:31) and others.

Angels minister in conveying messages from the throne of God to all the plains within and without the golden city, our witnesses tell us.

Judging from the especially revealed order on the plain in the city of the Infant Paradise, the place where infants are first nurtured and trained, we get marvelously illuminating insight into the perfect system of angelic ministry in heaven. Marietta Davis was led to heaven to receive particularly an insight into the plan of ministry among infants. By Jesus himself she was told to make these things known on earth. She was given comprehensive insight into the angelic ministry in one of the infant homes of the lowest order.

One angel of high rank presided over that home. Its face and body radiated the brightest light, the manifestation that is in proportion to rank and power. Working harmoniously with this head angel were seven others somewhat less in power and radiant light and life. Each of these seven, in turn, had loving charge of seven other angels somewhat lower in power and radiance.

Each angel in this lower rank was in charge of a class of "guardian angels" each of whom nurtured and developed the unfolding life of an infant in her charge. In this one home fifty-six angels gladly obeyed directions from angels of higher rank as they served those of lower order than themselves.

The whole system finally reached its real objective in its ministration to forty-nine groups of maturing infants in this one home, each child having its own specially assigned guardian angel. In this final delegation the angels assigned to nourish each particular child were especially suited to give the best care to the infant in its developing nature.

Angels returning from earth and bringing in their arms infants who had just died, upon reaching the infants' home in Paradise, gave over the children to other angels in the home whose duty it was to care for the new arrivals. The infants in the charge of these guardian angels were later passed on to more advanced homes on the same infant plain and so on until at last they reached the great central home on this plain. From there, in time, these children were advanced to begin again in the outer, or lower, grade of the next higher plain, and then from home to home and plain to plain, "from glory to glory", as we have already shown.

It can be seen at once that all this angelic order is in accord with the principles of God. He is a "God of order." His system is so perfect that not a sparrow falls without His notice.

Each child in heaven has its angel instructor and guide in each school of spiritual development, as it passes from school to school in Infant Paradise. The very touch of the angel's hand is a quickening life-touch.

Man in his highly organized business affairs and in his governments on earth finds it possible to effect his ends by very careful organization. But man's systems are far from perfect. His plans must be executed by erroneous, imperfect men. At best, man's careful systems of government are but a dim, distorted shadow of the perfect government of the kingdom of God, where not a detail is wrongly planned by God or imperfectly executed by the angels.

It is needless to add that the same perfect order as that in Infants' Paradise prevails under angelic supervision and ministry on all the countless plains below and without and within the city of the King. From the lowest sphere to the palace of the King there is not a place, a person, or a thing that does not move entirely in the will and purposes of God, directed and guided by His angels, whose directions issue from the throne.

We cannot know all the means the angels use in teaching, developing and enlarging those in their charge. Some things, however, have been made clear. Light as life-giving rays emanates from every angel. Those of lesser power and life among the redeemed, upon whom shines this angelic light and life, are thus quickened and endued. Intellectual capacities are enlarged. Thought is given greater range. Eyes are opened to behold greater stretches of heaven's plains, to see more of Eden's wonders. Association with the angels increasingly "tunes in" the spiritual natures of the redeemed to perceive deeper and higher realities.

The touch from the angel's hand is the touch of electrifying power that enlivens and flows through the developing loved one in the angel's charge, quickening to higher life and added strength. The sweetness in the angel's smile and the love tones in the angel's voice are constant causes of enlarging heart capacities in the one upon whom he constantly lavishes his special affection.

As the angels are embodiments of light and life, so are they personified music. Every step, every movement of an angel is music. There is music in his voice, music in the rhythm of his walk, and every motion of hand or body moves to heaven's music. From the lowest homes in Paradise to the palaces near the King, while serving, the angels everywhere sing. Golden harps and other finest stringed instruments angel fingers gently touch, producing music finer than mortals ever hear. The constant chord of heavenly music that floats through every home and place of instruction helps bring in tune with higher harmonies the expanding natures of all who are in the angels' care.

Perfect music sung and played by the angels helps bring the one-time-untuned and unstrung pilgrim from earth into higher and higher realms of ecstatic joy, divine peace and eternal harmony. Expanding souls, under the song of angels' harp and voice, grow from glory to glory in surpassing beauty until they become parts of perfect symphonies like the songs so pure and varied sung around the throne of God.

Although each angel and every saint sings praises from his own individual heart, there are also times of united singing and instrumental music. In the various wards and parks are vast temples, vast beyond any of man's construction, in which at intervals the heavenly inhabitants of the homes and mansions in the respective wards meet together for services of united song, worship and praise.

From the temples, or domes, multitudes of angels sing to the music of stringed instruments, while throngs of the blood-washed children of God join the heavenly choir in numberless parts as varied as the instruments the angels play; yet, every note is exactly tuned so that it adds to the one great harmony that rises like the sound of many waters. All this volume prepares for the already mentioned seasons of song when in all the heavenly parks, in all the planes of the golden city, praise spontaneously bursts forth from every temple, from every mansion, and from every heart in all the New Jerusalem. Joining the ten thousand angel harps and trumpets, and ten thousand times ten thousand, and thousands of thousands of angels is the mingled song of the great multitude that no man can number, gathered out of the tribulations and hardships of earth. All these together with all the angels who have had part in teaching them the ways of heaven, thus with one accord, burst forth in united praise of Him to whom is all power, all glory, all dominion forever more.

Beautiful schools of instruction under the direction of angels and saints from higher plains and great tabernacles for worship, exceeding all earthly architecture in size and grandeur, are parts of heaven's plains.

In summary, we see that the "innumerable hosts of angels" (Heb.12:22) in the New Jerusalem are appointed in such a way that every inhabitant of heaven has the constant ministry of angels to instruct him in the mysteries of redemption, the ways of heaven and the unfathomed things of eternity.

We see also that in the instruction and development of man redeemed from earth, the music of the angels is a constant part of God's plan to bring the spiritual natures of men into the highest harmonies of heaven.

ANGELS SERVE IN HEAVEN

Angelic hosts of every rank,
On every shore and river bank:
In every park, on every plain,
With Christ and saints in heaven reign.

In all the realms of God above,

In working out His plans of love:
In every mansion, come and go
The angels, whom the inmates know.

With harp and song in one accord,
The angels' music helps afford:
A chorus, that all heaven moves,
To harmonies the Lord approves.

The angels radiate a light
That's as the sun, or still more bright—
Which varies as the angels' power,
That differs, such as star from star.

From Infants' School and Paradise,
To highest schools in highest skies:
The angels help each understand
The order of all heaven's land.

They teach and guide, and lead each one,
In brighter light to near the throne:
To stand at last on highest plain,
In Jesus' stature to remain.

WITH THE ANGELS IN THEIR CITY

Hark! Listen to the angels sing
Their praise to Christ, the conquering King!
While saints, in parks and mansions fair,
Join with this chorus in the air
And birds of beauty in the trees
Unite with angels' jubilees.
The children, resting from their play,
Take part in this angelic lay;
The hills and mountains music make,
And echo back across the lake
The anthems of the angels sweet,
That lay all praise at Jesus' feet.

Thus every park on every plain
Joins in the angels' glad refrain
As angels float o'er mansions fair
In heaven's golden, balmy air.
The saints of old, from Able's day,
Take part in this angelic lay;
Where all who ever enter in

This glory land where is no sin,
Are clothed with heaven's garments new
In robes of every shade and hue.

There's not a park, or mansion fair,
Whose life the angels do not share;
They mingle with the holy men
Who one time lived in worldly sin.
They walk with saints in parks above
They talk with them of Jesus' love;
They saunter by the brooks and dells,
Or dancing where the flowers shed
A thousand perfumes round their head;
They join the youthful atmosphere
That is the lot of all up there
Where saints today, with saints of yore,
Rejoice and dance forever more.

In pastures green and on the lawns
Where feed the deer and play the fawns,
The angels, with their snowy feet,
Unharmful tread on flowers sweet
And touch the jeweled, silver string,
To help the songs the children sing.

A PILGRIM'S WELCOME BY THE ANGELS

Midst flowers fair, by crystal stream,
There sits a saint who seems to dream;
For he can scarce believe his eyes,
That he has come to higher skies.
An angel comes on him to smile,
And sit by him to talk awhile;
This pilgrim, from the earth below,
Had never thought that he could know
The joys that thrill and fill him there,
When angels sit by him so near.

He never felt so free before
To talk about the things of yore,
As when the angel held his hand
And said that he could understand
The motives, and the ways of men,
Who now, in heaven, live again.

Though now he wore his robes of snow,
The pilgrim said he did not know
The secrets of the life above,
Where all is one united love.
He'd just arrived in city fair,
From where he left a life of care;
He'd never had a half a chance
In heaven's knowledge, to advance
Like many others who were free
To spend more time in prayer than he.

The angel clasped his hand again,
And said, "We're glad you have come in
To join us in this heaven life,
Where never comes a care, or strife.
You're not a stranger-pilgrim here,
For thousands now await to cheer
You as you now, a victor come,
To live in this eternal home.

Oh, can't you hear the trumpet sound
And blares of bugles all around?
As now they come to welcome you
As one who to your Lord was true?
The pilgrim saw in distant skies,
A cloud of glory as pure light
That spread beyond his farthest sight.
When now, it came afloating near,
He could the songs of angels hear
And see the hosts of saints in white,
Whose faces shone with glory bright.

As rank on rank, they now came down,
With each a gemmed and golden crown:
They gathered 'round the pilgrim there,
Who sat beside the angel fair
And with their silver trumpets blew
The silver notes, that well he knew,
Were those that welcome victors home,
Who on the earth, have overcome.
The hosts of angels then begun
And joined by saints concordant sung
The victors' song, in one accord,
For him who'd used the Spirit's sword.

"We welcome thee, come from below,
Washed in the blood as white as snow!"
The saints and angels joyous sang,
As through the realms of heaven rang
This triumph song the angels raise
To every faithful warrior's praise.

An angel, who the angels led,
Then stepped out from the host and said:
"The record you have made on earth
Begun the day of your new birth,
Is written in our records here;
And in what's written doth appear
The motives that were in your heart
From which your actions had their start.
Within the book, that bears your name,
An angel looked the day you came
And found it written, bold and clear,
That you had lived in Jesus' fear;
And that you loved Him, most of all,
Who'd died to lift you from your fall.
Now, we have come at His command
To welcome you with clasp of hand
To join us in this land of bliss,
Where we, and all, are always His."

CHAPTER 11
SAINTS SERVING IN HEAVEN

"His servants shall serve Him." (Rev. 22:3). Saints in heaven are those who served the Lord upon earth. They served Him then in higher spheres, in higher service they minister to Him now. The greatest privilege of saints on earth or in heaven is to serve Him to whom they owe their all.

A "cloud of witnesses" were shown that all the redeemed in heaven are ever busy in happy service. While details of this service are not fully revealed, yet, for the encouragement of dwellers upon the earth, the Lord was pleased to make known some of the glorious ministry in which those who have gone on before us have a blessed part.

We have plenty of testimony that glorified saints from higher plains in heaven at times descend to help in the instruction of those on lower plains, and these, in turn, help on plains still lower. Thus there is a mutual system of cooperative instruction whereby those in advanced plains, mansions and temples of instruction help those below, the more advanced helping the less advanced throughout all the plains in the third and the second heaven. All is one great, inter-related co-operation, one great school of millions where all are teachers and all are pupils. Here every service is joyfully offered. Nor is there jealousy, or so much as an envious thought on the part of those in less advanced degrees of progress. Those below rejoice with joy unfeigned in every blessing experienced by the more advanced saints. They "rejoice with those who rejoice." On the other hand, every service is rendered in humble love and full-hearted thankfulness for being allowed to pass on to others blessings received there. Saints, like angels, are endued with life from the throne. By this life they are enabled to help develop in a larger measure those advancing to higher heights.

Not only do saints from higher plains have access to plains below them, but at times, for lessons in higher truth, those lower are led for short seasons to visit higher temples, higher mansions and higher plains above. This, we may suppose, is somewhat like a teacher with a class in a lower department of a factory. He might for a day take his pupils through the highly specialized departments of the factory to allow them to see the finished product, thus enabling them to get a more comprehensive grasp of the whole plan in which they are having, as yet, but a small part. At the same time, these pupils would necessarily have to return to their daily instruction, thence later to advance from department to department to the highly specialized department for permanent residence and instruction. From the new arrival whose work is of a lower grade to the most skilled expert in the highest department, each and everyone in the whole factory has his own individual work to do. All is necessary work. Not a man, or an item, could be spared in making the finished work, when assembled in the highest room, a perfect product.

Young tribesmen at Bible study. They help one another in love, without envy or pride. It is so in heaven. Those on higher plains in humility help those on lower plains.

Thus also, from the latest arrival who enters its service to the saints who have become heaven's experts through the ages spent in advancing from plain to plain and glory to glory there is not an unimportant piece of work. Nor is there a saint, no matter how inexperienced on earth, who will not have some part, larger or smaller, in the one great plan. No one will covet another's work. No one will feel his work useless. Everyone will be advanced to higher degrees of service as fast as he can do the higher work. Preparation on earth enables saints in heaven to enter as high service as they are qualified to do, just as a student from school can enter as skilled a department of work as his preparation will allow.

As on earth saints help one another to advance in the things of God, so in heaven. Work begun on earth will continue in heaven. There saints will help saints. Those above will help those below. On earth some are pastors, some evangelists, some apostles, some prophets, for the building up of the saints until they come to a perfect building in the Lord, rightly fitted together.

Tribes women in the province of Yunnan, China, helping one another in Bible study. The more advanced help those on lower plains of knowledge of the things of the kingdom of God. It is so in heaven; mutual love, mutual ministry.

In heaven saints also help saints. If the work of saints on earth is, as we believe, a dim fore-shadow of the work of saints in heaven, there will be manifold phases of heavenly work. Not all are pastors, not all are preachers, not all are evangelists on earth, not everyone is especially qualified to do the diverse work of all these in building up the saints in the spiritual building of the Lord. Yet in heaven will there not be those who will continue the work they began, but could not complete upon earth? Must not immature Christians who leave the present life in a low state of Christian development be built up in the deeper things of God after they get to heaven? And will not this service be done through the teaching of saints as well as of angels, especially qualified for this particular ministry in heaven?

Visitors to heaven say it is so. In heaven one saw missionaries, each surrounded by a little group whom God had enabled her to win to Himself from some darkened corner of the earth. She saw one "missionary standing in the midst of a group of African children whose little black faces were radiant with light and glory." Among those so ministering she noticed that: "It seemed that those who had suffered most for Jesus' sake, those who had 'come up out of great tribulation', were the ones whose faces shone with the most glory and heavenly light.'"

Here I work with men of various tribes, teaching them the Bible. Will I not, on one of heaven's plains, continue this work that at best I do so imperfectly here?

Another describes a scene in heaven: "As we passed onward, in looking down we began to see many suburban villages similar to that in which our own happy homes (heavenly) were situated. Among many of them there was an unfamiliar air, and the architecture of the buildings in many respects seemed quite different from our own. We soon realized what caused the apparent difference in the architecture and surroundings. Where our homes were situated (in heaven) we were surrounded by people we had known and loved on earth and of our own nationality.

"Many of these villages we found were formed from what, to us, would be termed foreign nations, and each village retained some of the peculiarities of its earth-life, and these, to us, were unfamiliar. We recognized again the goodness of the Father in thus allowing friends of the same nationality to be located near each other in heaven as on earth.

"We saw a group of people seated upon the ground in a semi-circle. They seemed to be hundreds in number, and in their midst a man was standing who apparently was talking to them. Something familiar, and yet unfamiliar, in the scene attracted us and I said, 'Let us go nearer and hear, if possible, what he is saying, and see who these people are.'

Upon doing this we found the people resembled in a great measure our own Indian tribes, and their dress, in a manner, corresponded to that worn on earth, though so etherealized as to be surpassingly beautiful; but, the dusky faces and the long black hair still remained. The faces, with intense interest depicted on each, were turned toward the man who, we could see, was talking to them. Looking upon him we saw at once that he belonged to the Anglo-Saxon race. In a whisper of surprise I said to my sister: 'Why, he is a missionary!'

"As so often it seemed to me to happen in that experience, when a surprise, or a difficulty, presented itself there was always someone near to answer and enlighten us. And so we found on this occasion that our instructor was beside us ready to answer any surprise, or question, that might be asked. He said at once:

"'Yes, you are right. This is a missionary who gave his life to what on earth were called the heathen. He spent many years in working for them and enlightening those who sat in darkness, with the result, as you see before you, of bringing hundreds into the kingdom of the Master; but, as you will naturally suppose, they have to learn, and here he still gathers them about him, and day by day leads them higher and higher into the blessed life.'

"'Are there many such', I asked, 'doing this work in this beautiful realm?'

"'Many hundreds', he said. 'To these poor minds, unlightened as they were when they first came, heaven, where they are in lower plains, is as beautiful and happy a place; as it is to any who have ascended higher, simply because we can enjoy only in the capacity to which our souls can reach. There are none of us who have not much yet to learn of the wonderful country.'

"In several instances we heard songs of praise arising from the temples and from people collected in different ways. And in many cases, to our surprise, the hymns and the words were those with which we had been familiar on earth and, although sung in a strange language, we under stood them all. That was another of the wonderful surprises in heaven. There was no language that we could not understand."

In paradisiacal centers are magnificent temples in which at times those who inhabit that particular part of heaven's vast domain gather for worship, adoration and praise; and where they are inspired and helped by the preaching of the Lord's choicest saints who have reached higher spheres of development in the kingdom of heaven.

Why should not missionaries in heaven continue to bring to higher degrees of consummation work they have begun on earth? And why should not these native peoples in at least their early stages of heavenly life retain some of their racial characteristics? Upon the New Earth there will be nations, for of the New Jerusalem, its capital, it is written: "The nations of them which are saved shall walk in the light of it and the kings of the earth do bring their glory and honor into it." (Rev. 21:24). May not those who occupy plains without the city still retain some racial features and bring their glory into it? All are, of course, free from racial prejudices and pride and respect of persons. In any case, all who come from every race and tribe and tongue are of different appearance, it seems, yet harmonious members of the one family of God.

All thoughts, as we have said, are intuitively known in heaven, whether expressed in heaven's universal language, or spoken in any earthly language, or not expressed in language at all.

All these considerations bring rapture to me. As part of my service for my Lord over in that fairer land may I not have the privilege of more perfectly teaching those I have so imperfectly taught on earth? In mingling with those in heaven with whom I worked on earth, may I not learn from them many things about the works of God, as I now do? In all the work among these heathen peoples there is so much to be done, so many to be instructed, so much to be taught in leading them out of darkness into higher and better understanding of the truths of God. Who is equal to all this? No missionary, or any number of native co laborers. But the work begun on earth that enables these peoples to become citizens of the heavenly kingdom must be continued in heaven by the saints and angels there. Shall I there again meet these dusky people among whom I now live and with whom I pray and with whom I study the wonders of redemption? Shall we meet again on the mountain tops of glory, or on the plains, or in the mansions of heaven to continue our development by searching into the unending riches of Christ? Together on that far-away shore in that balmier clime shall we again sing praises to our King?

We meet in our annual convention on earth. The future citizens of heaven come from various tribes, each in the dress peculiar to his tribe and each with his own facial characteristics; but, when we pray together, sing together, weep together at the foot of the cross, and the Holy Spirit falls in our midst, we are molded into one. We are one in heart. Though many, yet we are one.

Each tribe has its own peculiar dress. A heavenly visitor observed that in heaven those who came from different races and tribes retained some distinct characteristics of their earthly life and customs in dress. All this, however, was spiritualized and glorified to conform to the perfect order in heaven's Paradise.

Shall we not have a jubilee convention sometime in the land of cloudless day when numbers of our converts on earth will be there in the dress, facial coloring, and some earthly aspects of the Poo Maw, the La Lo, the Bee Yoh, the Buy E, the Ka Do and the Shien Tang tribes ? I believe so.

Already I have a little foretaste of blessings in service that, by foresight, I see on the sunny shore just over the river. On this side of the quiet river we gather together from different races and tribes and tongues. We study the Word of the Lord together; we wait upon God for enlargement of spiritual capacities through the Holy Spirit; and we prepare ourselves for more efficient service in preaching the glad tidings to the lost and in shepherding Jesus' sheep.

We recall our first gathering years ago when these men from various heathen tribes had just emerged from the forests and mountain fastnesses of heathen darkness. In the past they had never heard of God. They did not know were was a heaven; but, now they had just heard the glorious news. They had found Jesus, or rather, Jesus had found them. They had been washed in the blood of the Lamb, leaving them whiter than snow. They had become citizens of the heavenly kingdom of light, and they were clothed in robes of the King's righteousness. Yet, when we all met together for those first periods of study and preparation, how much did these newly adopted citizens of heaven know about the mysteries of the life and government of the heavenly country into which they had been translated out of life-long ignorance ?

After some years they still came to study the things of God, to learn more of His mysteries, to search deeper into His profound truths, and to seek deeper works of the Holy Spirit. At first young men came, and now young women also come. It is glorious to see them gathering together. Here they come down this mountain trail, or winding along that little mountain stream, or up that narrow valley.

As they meet their brown eyes sparkle and their brown faces almost radiate light. They are brothers and sisters in Christ, redeemed and made one in Him. True, they are from different tribes and tongues. They are the Poo Maws, Ka Dos, Bee Ees, La Los, Lo Los, Hsien Tangs, Koo Tsongs and Boo Kos.

At the feet of Jesus on the cross we weep and rejoice together. Although of many tribes with differing characteristics inherently, we are, nevertheless, one in Christ. In heaven it will still be so — many and different, and yet ONE.

Each tribe has its own language that they speak at home. Each has its own characteristic tribal attire; but, when they meet, the love of Christ makes them one in heart.

Who could teach them? How could it be done, for each one is in a class by himself? God can do it, and these tribal people participate in the doing by serving one another. As the language in common is the universal language of the country in which they live, the Chinese language, it is fairly well understood by these tribesmen, though not by the women. Some of the men can read the Bible in Chinese, though at first they do not understand it. Some cannot read at all and others can speak but little of the Chinese language. Some are quick to learn, and others with duller minds learn more slowly.

There is, in all, such a diversity that for perfect instruction there would need to be almost as many classes and as many teachers as there are pupils.

Now here is where it becomes heaven-like. Jesus moves in the midst of these people, pours out the Holy Spirit upon them, quickens dull minds and puts in their open, unpretentious humble hearts a hunger for more knowledge of God and His kingdom. All are eager to learn. All with full hearted diligence and single-hearted application study the Word.

When divided into classes those most advanced teach those less advanced. But this class study is not sufficient, for each individual has his own needs and no two make exactly the same progress. So they help one another. Those who know a little more help those who know a little less. One who forgets a written Chinese character asks one who knows it. One who does not understand the meaning of a verse of Scripture goes for help to someone who can explain it.

When we cross to the sunny land on the other shore we will continue our course with racial differences in color and ways that still continue from our earth life, with all that detracts from the glory of the Lord washed away in the river of life.

This is all a volunteer work done for Jesus' sake because of what He has done for us. No one gets any pay. All are here to learn to minister. I never notice anyone less advanced jealous of one more advanced. Nor have I ever seen the advanced unwilling to help the less advanced. Sometimes the more enlightened in the knowledge of the Lord are kept so busy helping others that they have little time for their own study. Since they sometimes, at a sacrifice, leave their families and home duties to come, I have thought they might be discontented at being kept busy giving when they came to receive. It is not so. If the Lord gives them a chance to study more, they do it with an eagerness and earnestness that is from heaven. If, however, they see it necessary to help by teaching, they do it joyfully as unto the Lord.

In all this I am taught some of the best lessons about heaven that I have ever learned. In trying over and over to teach some truth to a mind unable to grasp it, my Anglo Saxon disposition tires. When all are busy I look around and take lessons. Over there is a Poo Maw explaining something to a Ka Do who finds it hard to understand. He repeats it over and over with such patience and real heart interest that, as I look on, I meditate: "I wonder if God sent me here to have these tribal people teach me to be a real loving Christian, or if I am sent to teach them."

Regardless of tribes and tongues their spirit of helpfulness and their never-tiring zeal to acquire, or impart, knowledge of heaven's ways have wrought spiritual wonders in my own life. In teaching, I am taught; and they, in serving one another, are in turn served. And thus they learn the meaning of the Bible, thus they grow in spiritual life, and thus I see them, along with myself, growing "from glory to glory' right before my eyes here in these remote mountains. All this is "like heaven to me."

Shall we not thus in heaven help one another? Would I not be disappointed could I not in park, or temple, there gather with the Ka Dos, and Lo Los, and La Los, and Boo Kos and others still retaining some racial distinguishing marks and together again study further under better circumstances the unfathomed mysteries of God? Shall we not again sing on that other shore the songs of redeeming love, perhaps in Chinese language which we all understand, as well as sing in the universal language of heaven?

After each period of study in preparation for better service when in heaven, shall we not return each to his own home in the forests and parks among those of our own people in glory land where each "feels at home?"

As flowers differ in the order of heaven, so do saints. Each functions in the place the Lord appoints, shedding fragrance and inspiration without any jealousy of any other.

When I am among the natives I never feel perfectly "at home." Their lower standard of living does not fully satisfy me. On the other hand, when these people come to my house to study with me they do not feel "at home." Our flowers and shrubs and different standard of living mean little to these crude people from the mountains. In their lives of toil and lack of heavenly enlightenment they have never learned to appreciate the beautiful.

When, from a trip to the villages, I return to our own little home of flowers and simple natural beauties I sense a refreshing uplift that makes me "feel at home." Likewise, when these tribal people return to their homes from periods of study, they are elated when they enter their own unembellished environment and they have a happy sense of again being "at home." So it is in heaven. Each has his mansion where he will feel "at home."

These Ka Do tribal people feel "at home" in this environment, destitute of beauty. They would not at once feel at home in a mansion of high development of the beautiful. In heaven the "at home" adjustment will be arranged correctly, according to capacity to appreciate.

Yet, in spite of all these differences, a common fellowship here in our work on earth makes us all one, and the unions and constant reunions in the Lord make the love bonds between us stronger than the bonds between race or tribe, or brother or sister, or father or mother. Jesus' life in all unites us in one family. All the children of varied individuality look and act much like Father.

Not all are missionaries, not all are preachers, and not all are teachers. Not all exclusively do work of this nature on earth. In heaven it is the same. Each has his own labor of love, but not all are preachers there. Besides preaching, our tribesmen have many home duties, and their Christian wives and children have their daily work which is not teaching or preaching. So in heaven, each has his work. This much is clearly revealed, though the nature of this diversified labor we shall know only when we reach that beautiful land.

Will some of the artistic saints in heaven be busy preparing garments for those who are soon to arrive? Will some joyfully help in building mansions and embellishing them with jewels without the sound of hammer, or any debris? One saw it so. "His servants serve Him" in heaven serving others, those above helping those below in countless ways that heaven alone will make known to each of us in turn.

One great difference will characterize the service of saints in heaven from that of saints on earth. In heaven all work will be done in the fullness and the power of the Holy Spirit. Every word spoken by "pastor" or "teacher", or saint, will be in the Spirit. Every ear that listens to instruction will be a perfectly attuned ear, every heart an enlarged, Holy-Spirit-filled heart. Every ministry will always be in the ecstatic joy that perfect fullness of the Holy Spirit in heaven brings.

Thus in perfected holy life in the Holy-Spirit-fullness will saints in heaven join the angels in never-tiring, never-ending, perfectly happy, perfectly joyful ministry in the heavenly kingdom of God.

SAINTS SERVING IN HEAVEN

On earth, the saints have just begun
The service they will carry on
When each shall reach the golden shore,
Where saints shall serve forever more.
When we shall leave our bodies here,
As angels, by our bed, appear

To take us to the realms above,
Where all is always only love.

And as we arrive in heaven's land,
We then, at once, will understand
That, how we served our fellow men,
Since we, on earth, did once begin,

Prepares us now to serve on still
And higher purposes fulfill,
In helping other saints of God
To reach the fullness of the Word.

From higher plains and mansions there,
And higher schools each one will share
In helping others, by his love,
To progress to the plains above.

The best of saints so little know
When first, from earth to heaven they go,
That, step by step, they must be taught
The wonders which the cross has wrought.

With love, each one, will then impart
The love and truth within his heart
And in this love will each partake,
What he receives for Jesus' sake.

CHAPTER 12
ANGELS SERVING ON EARTH

"Are they not all ministering spirits sent forth to minister," is written of the services of angels on earth. To write of all the ministry of angels to saints in Bible days would be to rewrite a good share of the Bible.

ANGELS IN BIBLE DAYS

The law, the basis of all the Old Testament, was given to Moses through the ministry of angels. (Gal. 3:19). When the children of Israel were led out of Egyptian bondage, escaping across the Red Sea between the walls of water, the angel of the Lord went before them, leading the way to freedom. (Ex. 23:29). And the angels of heaven never ceased their ministry to God's chosen Israel: in times of adversity angels from above came with strong hands to deliver. Angels brought renewed courage to God's disheartened people. Israel, surrounded by enemies, was led to victory by the angels.

Angels ministered to men and talked with them. Angels talked and ate with Abraham. (Gen. 18). Angels spent a night in Lot's home, and taking him by the hand, led him to safety when destruction from heaven was about to fall. An angel brought food from Paradise for hungry, discouraged Elijah, food so nourishing that the prophet went for forty days in the strength of it, and the angel encouraged him to renew his battle for righteousness. Thousands of angels came to deliver Elisha. When Daniel was cast into the lions' den an angel from God shut the lions' mouths. (Dan. 6:22). From his own experience David wrote: "The angel of the Lord encampeth round about them that fear Him and delivereth them." (Ps. 34:7).

The New Testament, as well, is a record of the ministry of angels. An angel announced to Mary that she was to mother the Savior of the world, and when the Christ was born angels sang around the shepherds in Bethlehem hills. In the wilderness, where the beasts of earth and Satan with his powers of hell were, angels came to minister unto Jesus. When in Gethsemane the enemy came like a flood to crush Him before He reached the cross, angels descended to strengthen Him. (Lk. 22:43).

Angels bright as lightning rolled the stone away and Christ arose. The earth shook, the rocks were rent, the enemy guards about the tomb fell as dead men. Angels as God's messengers carry God's power and authority. They bring resurrection life to the sons of God, His heavenly family.

After His death on the cross and His burial, angels had a ministry in raising Jesus from the dead. They came to roll the stone away. In shining garments they sat on the stone and also sat where the Savior's body had been, telling the women, "He is risen from the dead."

After the Lord ascended on high to prepare a place for His people, angels continued to minister to men on earth. An angel appeared to Cornelius directing him to find Peter. Angels delivered saints from prison, angels directed Paul and Peter and others. An angel opened the prison door and delivered Peter from his bonds. In New Testament days angels so clearly helped in building up the churches that Paul had to write to some uninstructed Christians warning them not to worship the angels.

When the curtain goes down on the last Bible scene we see an angel leading up into heaven the disciple whom Jesus loved. Angels there gave him revelations to write in a book, the last book of the Bible, and told him what he wrote he was to send to "all the churches." (Rev. 7).

Briefly, then, the first book of the Bible was written by Moses who walked in fellowship with the angels. The Bible throughout records the ministry of angels, and it ends with a book directly given by angels for all the churches. The last Bible word is from the angels to men whom they serve on earth: "I Jesus have sent mine angel to testify unto you these things in the churches." (Rev. 22:16).

Angels Minister Yet

Angels will continue to minister on earth as long as the Lord's church remains on earth, for "are they not all ministering spirits, sent forth to minister for all who shall be heirs of salvation?" (Heb. 1:14). God's people still have God's angels to serve them and to minister unto them. We each have our guardian angels, our personal guards, and the little children have their angels who behold the face of the Father in heaven. (Matt. 18:10). In addition to our guardian angels, if need be, our Father in heaven can still send legions of angels to deliver those who love Him. The continued ministry of angels is so assured that it would be as easy to believe that God would cease to care as to believe that angels would cease to minister. Yes, they are servants of the Lord sent from glory to serve Him and in ministration lead us into the Promised Land.

Angels May Be Visible Or Invisible

Angels are "spirits", spiritual beings. Although usually invisible to the mortal eye, they sometimes manifest themselves in forms visible to the mortal eye, they some times manifest themselves in forms visible to men. In visible form the three angels appeared to Abraham and Sarah and talked and ate with them. (Gen. 18). Manoah and his wife also saw an angel. (Judges 6:8-21). In the New Testament instances already mentioned the ministries of angels were visible.

One person's spiritual eyes may be opened to see the angels around him while another at the same time may be blind to the angels' presence, as for instance, when Elisha saw the heavenly hosts of angels while his servant neither saw them nor perceived their presence. (2 Kings 6).

Angels Minister in Bringing the Holy Spirit

Angels coming down to earth bring some of heaven down. They come from God. They serve Christ in the land of light and life. Filled with His light and life, they carry heavenly life wherever they go.

As recorded in my earlier book, Visions Beyond the Veil, at the time of the outpouring of the Holy Spirit those "in the Spirit" often saw the angels about us. They sometimes saw an angel of greater power above the room of Spirit-filled children, while other angels circled the room or moved in our midst. In our own experience as well as that of others with whom I am acquainted, at times of special outpourings of the Holy Spirit, spiritually quickened eyes, under the anointing, see angels about them. It is apparent, then, that angels have a part in ministering the Holy Spirit to God's people on earth. Although the Holy Spirit and the glory of God Himself may fill a temple, as the glory from heaven filled the temple Solomon built, (2 Chron. 7). it also appears certain that angels, filled with the Holy Spirit and radiating the life of Christ as ambassadors of Christ, can and do help impart the Holy Spirit to souls on earth.

When the baptized Christians of Samaria had not received the Holy Spirit the church at Jerusalem sent "Peter and John who, when they were come down, prayed for them that they might receive the Holy Spirit . . . . Simon saw that through the laying on of hands the Holy Ghost was given." (Acts 8:16-18). In like manner Ananias laid his hands on Paul that he might "be filled with the Holy Ghost", (Acts 9:17). and Paul later laid his hands upon the twelve Ephesian Christians, and "the Holy Ghost came upon them." (Acts 19:6).

Angels come down is heaven come down. They are filled with the Holy Spirit, their life is perfect life in the Holy Spirit, and thus they bring healing and gifts and fruits of the Holy Spirit to God's children on earth.

Likewise, if Holy Spirit-filled men thus can lay hands on saints, each of whom in order receive s the Holy Spirit, can not, and may not, holier and more Spirit-filled angels from heaven lay invisible hands upon saints, importing the Holy Spirit? When it was the Lord's order at times of special anointing I have laid my hands upon Christians and have seen the manifestation of the power of God upon each one as clearly as Simon "saw" it. One night in particular I thought an angel must be laying his hands on some Ka Do Christians that they might receive the Holy Spirit as in days of old. When a group of women were praying with closed eyes, the manifest power of God came upon one after another in successive order right down the row as clearly as though an angel, passing down the line, were laying his invisible hand upon them one by one. This was repeated two or three times. The angel's touch brings power of the Holy Spirit, we are told.

In a gospel meeting under this tree, when there was a mighty out-pouring of the Holy Spirit, angels were seen in our midst, flying hither and thither, while three angels were in our midst. Tribes people danced under the anointing of the Holy Spirit and sixty were moved upon with supernatural manifestations. If ever I felt that heaven came to earth it was that time. That same day, when these mountain tribes people were being baptized in water, angels were heard singing over them.

The very presence of an angel radiates the power of God. You can sense the power of God emanating from a spirit filled man of God. When Charles Finney, filled with the Holy Spirit, stepped into a spinning factory where the girls were busy at work, without his speaking a word one after another of the girls became so affected by the spirit they could not work. Eventually it became necessary to stop the machines (*Life of Finney*, p. 183).

Now if one Holy Spirit-filled man by his silent presence could so influence a group of busy people, could not an appeal in the midst of a group of believers by his very presence in silent power be the means of many receiving the Holy Spirit? I verily believe so.

Angels and Visions

Angels have part in bringing visions to men. An angel brought a vision to John. (Rev. 22:16). In a "vision" Cornelius saw an angel. In almost every vision referred to in this present volume an angel appeared. Apparently angels from heaven open the spiritual eyes of saints on earth, enabling them to see the glories of the other world, and the angels also take mortals from earth to heaven to see these glories.

Angels and Gifts of the Holy Spirit

Angels, doubtless, also have a ministry in helping impart "gifts" of the Holy Spirit. "The spirits of the prophets are subject to the prophets." (1 Cor. 14:32). Are not the "spirits" of the prophets angels, and do not angels have a part, sometimes, or always, in prophetic utterances? For the very reason that angels have a ministry to us through prophecies we are admonished to "try the spirits whether they are of God: because many false prophets are gone out into the world." (1 John 4:1). Here the comparison is between false prophecy given by evil "spirits", or demons, and true prophecy given by the good "spirits", or angels.

Then again, for Jesus' sake angels minister to us in helping heal our diseases. The written accounts of persons seeing an angel touching them and healing their diseases so many that it is unnecessary to repeat here.

When the Lord, on Mount Olivet, commissioned His disciples to "go into all the world and preach the gospel to every creature" He promised that part of their world-wide ministry to last throughout the age would be that believers shall "lay hands on the sick and they shall recover." (Mark 16:15-17). And Jesus said, "I am with you always, even unto the end of the world (age)." (Matt. 28:20).

In this village a half-grown Ka Do tribes-boy prayed for a sick Ka Do woman. The power of God suddenly came upon the boy in a mighty supernatural way, and the sick woman saw an angel. She was healed. Angels help in healing the sick and in the ministry of the Holy Spirit.

Since believers have a healing ministry throughout the age, do not the angels, through whom we get much of our power, have a much larger, though often invisible, ministry in healing the sick? Doubtless in many, perhaps most cases, the saint visibly lays hands on the sick and an invisible angel heals him, filling the sick with new life from the pure waters of life, flowing from the throne of God.

A half grown Ka Do tribal boy, visiting in a remote village, was asked by a sick woman, who had never heard of angels, to pray for her. As he prayed the power of God came mightily upon both the boy and the sick woman. The woman saw a bright angel with wings. She was healed. In many instances angels have been seen when the sick were divinely healed through prayer.

When this woman, one of our best Ka Do Christians, was seriously ill she saw heavenly hands laid upon her and she was healed. These could have been no other than the hands of an angel.

One of our best Ka Do Christian women had been very ill for some time. She appeared to be in great darkness, when a light from above descended upon her, and two light- radiating hands and arms appeared. One of these hands was placed under her shoulders. With these kindly arms she was gently raised into a sitting position. Her mother, who was near, was greatly surprised to see the sick woman suddenly arise and sit up. The woman was healed. On another occasion, when this same woman had been sick for a considerable time, two light-radiating hands were laid upon her and she was healed again. Were not these angel's hands? f not, whose?

Angels and Evil Spirits

We live on a battlefield. We are in the midst of the greatest war of the ages; as this age now draws to an end the fiercest battle of all time closes in around us. The great and terrific war among the nations is, after all, a small affair compared with the invisible conflict in the air between the angels of God and the angels and demons of Satan. This war, in our first heaven, is concerning the souls of men.

A stronger One than the enemy who holds captive the souls of men has come to set the captive free. The Victor has risen in triumph from the dead, Conqueror over Death, Hell and the Grave. He has ascended on high far above all principalities and powers and dominions. His victory shall prevail and His kingdom shall be set up, the everlasting kingdom of heaven that will be forever and forever. As the day of victory approaches the forces of the great usurper contend with fiercest rage.

Fiercest of all places that this conflict rages is in the air. So strongly are the forces of Satan entrenched in the heavens above the earth that Gabriel, an angel of highest power, for twenty days was withstood by a mighty prince of Satan. (Dan. 10).

This well-educated Christian friend of mine wrote to me how, at the time a bomb struck the Palace Hotel in Shanghai, where he and a friend were taking lunch, they heard a voice saying, "get under the table." He was saved, while people all around were killed. He believes an angel saved Him.

This conflict in the air continues unremittingly. Where the Lord works, there Satan's forces hinder. Where there are special movements of the Holy Spirit, there large detachments of fallen angels and demons are dispatched to oppose the work of God. Where angels work devils rage. All this is because of the war the powers of darkness press in their counter attack to recapture those who move toward God. Were it not for the individual guardian soldiers from heaven and the power of angels in resisting the evil spirits of Satan, who could hope successfully to press through the powers of the fiends and the demons of Satan to the Lord of eternal liberty?

But, in spite of all demoniacal resistance, heaven does come down to earth. The light of heaven does shine in earth's darkness. God's people do get guidance, for the angels from heaven bring heaven to us and they lead us to heaven's portals.

This well-educated Christian friend of mine wrote to me how, at the time a bomb struck the Palace Hotel in Shanghai, where he and a friend were taking lunch, they heard a voice saying, "get under the table." He was saved, while people all around were killed. He believes an angel saved him.

The Lord's angels protect His people from physical harm, for "the angel of the Lord encampeth round about them that fear Him, and delivereth them" (Ps. 34:7). and "He shall give His angels charge over thee, to keep thee in all thy ways." (Ps. 91:11). God is still alive. His angels still serve Him. His angels are still ministering spirits who come from heaven and camp round about them who are truly the children of God, born again of the Spirit.

An Angel Spake To Them

A foreign-educated Chinese friend of mine in Shanghai recently baptized in the Holy Spirit, wrote me what happened in Shanghai at the beginning of the war with Japan, when by mistake a Chinese plane dropped the bomb which ruined the Palace Hotel. He with some companions were eating lunch in a nearby hotel when the bomb exploded. A voice called, "Get under the table." These two no sooner got under the table than the ceiling collapsed, spreading ruin. When they went out into the street they found it strewn with corpses. They know it is true that "the angel of the Lord encampeth round about them that fear Him and delivereth them."

This friend in Sha ngh ai, a missionary, tells how in the beginning of the war unseen hands bodily lifted an old Chinese Christian woman out of the way of flying bullets several times, and enabled her to escape.

An Angel Moved Her Around

Shortly after this a missionary friend of mine was visiting a refugee camp. There she met a poor Chinese Christian woman whose heart was filled with overflowing praise for her miraculous deliverance by the angels. She was living in her humble shack in the Chinese section of Shanghai when it was attacked by the Japanese. At the time of the attack this Christian woman was in bed. A strong, unseen hand picked her up bodily, placing her in the corner of the room as bullets swept over her bed. Again this unseen power, picking her up, placed her in another part of the room as bullets penetrated the corner from which she was so miraculously removed. A third and fourth time she thus was moved until she was able to escape. Philip was picked up and bodily carried away in Bible days, (Acts 8:39) and God never lost His power since then. The messengers of Him who can move the mountains still camp round about them who fear Him and deliver them.

This friend in Shanghai, a missionary, tells how in the beginning of the war unseen hands bodily lifted an old Chinese Christian woman out of the way of flying bullets several times, and enabled her to escape.

Angels Stopped Japanese War Planes

Some months ago I read the account written by an American, long in China, who could speak Japanese as well as Chinese. In conversation with men of the Japanese air force he was told that one of their air men was dispatched to lead a number of planes in attacking a Chinese town. When nearing the town, his own plane leading, he suddenly saw a white cloud appear in the distance. As his plane neared the cloud he saw a group of angels. His plane became unsteady. Repeatedly he endeavored to direct his plane in the direction of the town, but the hindering cloud of angels made it so impossible to control his plane that he circled around and, followed by the others, returned to the base from which he started. Since he did not attack the town and the Japanese authorities did not believe in angels, the leader of this attacking plane was executed for disobedience.

The American who related this also got the other side of the story. In that town to be attacked, great apprehension was felt because of the impending danger, as an attack from airplanes was hourly expected. In that place was a little group of Chinese Christians led by a consecrated old Chinese pastor. In view of the imminent danger the pastor and his people gave themselves to praying to the God of Daniel. On the day of the attack the pastor was praying to Him who said He would give His angels charge over His people. The people in the town did not see the angels, but they saw the airplane in the lead circle around and return with the other planes following.

Those simple Chinese believe that the God who once sent an angel to close the lions' mouths can now send angels to stop an airplane in its flight.

Angels Push War Tanks Back

A few years ago a French acquaintance, a Catholic banker in Yunnanfu, China, told me that during the World War 1 (at the battle of Marne, if I remember correctly), his friends saw angels pushing back the German tanks. A great many saw this angelic help with the result that a number of his infidel friends became Christians. Yes; the angels are up-to-date. The angels who pushed down the walls of Jericho, and who some day will come back with Jesus to throw down the mountains, are now taking a part in the affairs of men. They are working out God's purposes, even among unbelievers; but, their special work is looking after the affairs of the heirs of salvation. Angels who in past times turned armies of aliens to flight (2 Kings 7:5,7) can now reverse the mad course of war planes and war tanks.

An old Chinese pastor and his people prayed in a Chinese town. The Japanese in the air planes were met by a cloud of angels who made it impossible to control the planes for further advance, and caused them to retreat.

Angels Delivered Missionaries and Christians

Mr. Jensen, a Danish missionary in this part of China, tells of some of his missionary acquaintances in North China. They, with their little group of Christians, were in very grave danger from the fighting about them. When gathered together for earnest prayer they saw an angel suddenly appear, standing on top of the mission building. The angel, turning this way and that way, looking from side to side, with clasped hands bowed in worship and then disappeared. The Christians were delivered.

An Angel Stopped a Motor and Saved a Man

Evangelist C— P— relates an angel story (*Golden Grain*, January, 1940). A good old Christian man, living in the country, on a cold January night was driving home from town. Snow was following in clouds, completely covering the tracks of the railroad that intercepted his way. Although the old man could see, his hearing was bad, and the snow obscured the things ahead and on all sides of him.

As he drove along in his "Model T Ford" toward the snow covered iron rails, his motor suddenly stopped, and his car stood still. Instantly an unseen and unheard train thundered past, just in front of the old saint of God, over whom the Lord had definitely promised that He would give His angels charge.

His motor was all right. He had plenty of gasoline. When the train passed, he started his motor and drove on to his own home, assured that, while we may not always see the angels, the angels always see us and are faithful to their charge.

Night came on, and a blinding snowstorm made it impossible to see the railroad ahead. The engine of the Ford suddenly stopped. An angel of the Lord must have stopped it, for just as the Ford came to this sudden standstill a night express train rushed in front of it over the track veiled by the storm of snow. There was no engine trouble; there was plenty of gas. The old saint of God, who alone rode in the Ford, started his engine and again continued his journey, thanking God for His angels.

ANGELS COME DOWN TO SERVE ON EARTH

Angels descend from the heavens above
To minister here unto men,
And bring heaven's light and spirit of love
To a world in the shades of sin.

They help in the work of saving the lost
Out of the darkness of night,
And in keeping the saved at the blood-bought cost,
Secure on the paths of right.

The holy touch of an angel's hand
On the fever-heated brow,
Restores the peace of the heavenly land
As a share of heaven now.

The Holy Spirit's gifts and powers,
That saints on the earth would know;
And other blessings, which are pure,
The angels help to bestow.

Angels are there, where the children play
By the streams on earthly shore,
To join their joy and guard their way

To the land of evermore.

Angels descend to save the Lord's own,
And minister day by day;

They help in danger; we're never alone:
They are listening when we pray.

They walk and they work and talk with men,
Who are pilgrims here below;
And escort to the land that is free from sin,
The saved, who their Savior know.

CHAPTER 13
ANGELS SERVING ON EARTH
(Continued)

Shall I tell some more about the angels? Let us talk about the angels. Let us tell our children and our children's children about the angels from heaven. These stories children like to hear, stories children's hearts in tune with heaven can believe. Do not the angels who minister to children always behold the face of the Father in heaven? (Matt. 18:10). Why, I often wonder, are the angels who minister to children especially mentioned as "beholding the face of the Father in heaven?" Can it be that Father is particularly glad to talk with the angels who care for the little ones of whom it is said, "Of such is the kingdom of heaven?"

Angels Kept a Little Boy From Freezing

One night in 1936, those listening over the radio in Angelholm, Sweden, heard the announcement that a little five-year old boy had been lost in a dense forest. It appears that a dog ran into the forest and the little boy, Rune, followed him. When the mother went to look for her child she could not find him in the forest, nor did he answer her calls. At first the father, with a few friends, hunted for Rune. They searched in vain all day long. The next day more men joined the searching party. In increasing numbers they came each day to help find the missing boy. After four or five days they all feared the child was dead from hunger and exposure to the intense cold of the nights in that Swedish forest.

On the sixth day nearly four hundred people joined the search in the pathless woods. Just as they were about to return home without hope the father's heart leaped with joy at the sound of his little son's voice not far from him. There, alive and well, sat the child on a little mound of moss. No one had believed that a child could live six days so exposed to hunger and cold. Yet the child was in good health. The doctor who examined him could find nothing wrong with him. The child told his rejoicing mother: "At night I looked up to the stars and prayed to God to help me get home again. One night I got cold, but the angel kept me from freezing." (Matt. 18:10).

An Angel Visited Five Children in Ohio

When I was in Shanghai a friend asked me if I had ever heard about the angel who visited some little children in Ohio, and she offered to copy the account from a typewritten record she had. When she gave me the copy another missionary friend, Miss Longstreth, said: "Why, I know all about that angel's visit. The children's parents told my parents all about it before the account was ever published. From what publication the account is copied I do not know, but that is unimportant, as I have the story verified by one who knows it to be true. I later had a friend visit the home of this angel's visit and had photos taken of the place and of some of those who saw the angel. The story is as follows:

"For the glory of God and the encouragement of His obedient children, I recall this bit of marvelous history, which occurred in the month of February, A. D., 1887, in the northern part of Dark county, Ohio.

"About three miles from Roseville there lives a man and his wife, by the name of John and Hattie Hittle. They had six children whose names and ages were as follows: Ora, twelve; Henry, ten; Lizzie, eight; Ida, six; Nettie, four, and Pearl, two.

"They were very religious people and enjoyed the blessing of sanctification. They were, and still are, members of the Massasinawa Class of Greenville Mission of the Indiana Conference of the Evangelical Association. Their home has for many years been the home of itinerant preachers.

"There was a protracted meeting in the neighborhood to which the parents and Ora were going while the rest of the children were to stay at home alone. They had never stayed alone before, and there protested it on the plea that they were afraid; but, the mother told them not to be afraid, for God and the angels would take care of them.

"Finally they consented, and after the parents were gone they lowered the blinds, locked the doors and gathered together on the sofa to have their family worship. Pearl had been put to sleep in the cradle in the bedroom. After they had all said their prayers they happened to get hold of the "Foster Child's Story of the Bible" which had been presented to Ora on his twelfth birthday. They began look-ing at the pictures, and presently came to the picture of an angel, whereupon Henry exclaimed:

"'Oh ! I wish I could see an angel once !'

"And the rest said, 'I wish I could, too !'

"They had hardly said this when they heard a sound on the porch as of a rustling of silk garments; then a knock on the door. So they all jumped up and ran to the door to see who was coming. They raised the curtain and looked out, and behold! To their surprise, an angel came right in through the door, or glass of the door, the latter being locked, and stood among them. He asked them where their parents were and they told him they had gone to meeting. Then Liz-zie, who happened to be standing by the rocking chair, said to him:

"'Take a chair and sit down.

"He answered, 'Oh, I can't stay long.' But he took the chair and drew it up toward the stove and sat down, saying as he did so:

" 'You have a nice stove and a good, warm fire.'

"Then the children noticed that he was bare-footed. As the weather was cold and the ground covered with snow, they would naturally suppose he must have cold feet. Therefore, Henry said to him:

"'Put your feet on the railing of the stove and warm them.'

"The angel did so, and then called the children to him. They were still wondering in their minds why he should be bare-footed in such cold weather, and this made them take particular notice of his feet, which looked perfectly white and glistened like wax.

"He then reached out his hands and took Ida on one knee and Nettie on the other, and caressed them by putting his hands on their heads as if he were blessing them. At the same time he kept talking to them all, telling them to be good children and keep on praying to God, etc. His voice was clear and charming, his hair fine and wavy, and he wore a beautiful little crown on his head.

"After he had held them awhile he put them down, and rising from the chair, began to walk around and look at the pictures on the wall. As he walked they noticed that his garments were loosely thrown about him and extended a little below his knees. They could now have a better opportunity to see his wings, which were quite large and fairly glittered for whiteness.

"The children followed him wherever he went, and presently they came to the bedroom, where Pearl was sleeping. With the children close at his side he went to the cradle and took Pearl in his arms and kissed her, and then laid her down again, saying as he did so:

"'When Pearl gets older you must tell her to be a good girl and pray, too.' Then he said to them: 'Well, I must go now', and began to shake hands with each one of them and thus bid them good-bye.

'It is impossible to describe the loveliness of his hand as they took hold of it. It felt like snow, or some downy cushion and, like his feet. it was perfectly white and glistening. He wore a most heavenly smile upon his countenance. His voice was tender and sweet. His entire demeanor was marked with gentleness and kindness, and his whole appearance was that of grandeur and beauty. They felt perfectly at home and enraptured with his presence, and it made them feel sad when he told them he must go.

"After he had bidden them good-bye, he started for the door, while the children were still standing at the bed-room door. When he came to the door he paused a moment, and the children noticed that he had a long staff in his hands, and in an instant they saw him gliding out through the unopened door in the same manner that he had come.

"As soon as they saw he was gone they instantly made a rush for the door, literally tumbling over one another to get there first, and they saw him standing on the edge of the porch, and a bright cloud had gathered about him. They saw him glide out into the yard. His body was now in an inclined position with his feet extending backwards and his wings partially folded, while the lower part of his garment and the bright cloud seemed to roll and fold themselves together in a unique manner. He went on in this way until he came half way between the house and a pear tree which was standing in the yard, and then he ascended, his beautiful white feet being the last thing they saw of him. Then one of the children exclaimed:

"'Now he is gone !'

"Another said: 'I wonder why there was no bright cloud around him while he was with us in the room.'

"Still another said: 'I wonder how long it will take him to get to heaven.'

"The next thing in order was to wait until the return of the parents and Ora that they might tell it to them. They could scarcely wait until they came, they were so anxious to tell them. In the meantime they carefully examined the door from top to bottom, rubbing their hands over it to see if there was not a crack, or a break, of some kind where he had come in and gone out; but, to their astonishment, they could not find the least sign of a crack either on the door, the glass, or on the casing of the door.

"After awhile they heard their parents coming and they were all up and ready to meet them. The mother went to the house first, while the father and Ora put away the team. Who can imagine the bustle and excitement as the mother entered the house. Henry, Lizzie, Ida and Nettie, each trying to tell it first. They jumped, they laughed, they clapped their hands and were perfectly wild with joy. So great was the noise and holy racket that the father and Ora heard them at the barn and wondered what in the world vas the matter with the children.

"'Who do you suppose was here, mother, while you were gone?' they all exclaimed with one accord. 'An angel, yes; an angel ! Oh ! Mother, an angel was here.'

"When the mother had quieted them sufficiently, they went on to describe him, how he looked, what he had said and what he had done.

"Their shining faces, their exultant spirits, their positive declarations, and the unison of their assertions soon overwhelmingly convinced the mother of the truthfulness of her children's story and of the reality of the vision which they had seen. Besides, being a spiritual woman and having an insight into spiritual things, she could the more easily be persuaded of the facts in the case. She listened with suppressed emotion until her heart could no longer contain the joy which filled and thrilled her whole being. Then, going to the bedroom she threw herself upon her bed and gave vent to her feelings with loud shouts of "Glory to God." She felt that the very house was hallowed by the presence of the Lord, and that from henceforth, more than ever, her home should be like a little heaven on earth. After rising from the bed she seated herself in a chair near the stove and buried her face in her hands.

"Presently the father and Ora returned from the barn and as they entered the room where she was sitting, she exclaimed:

"'Oh, Father! You ought to hear the children tell of the wonderful visitor they had while we were gone', where upon the children began to tell the story to their father and older brother.

"'Ah !' said the father: 'you are only excited; it is simply your imagination. You did not see an angel.'

"'Yes, yes—father; sure, sure', came from every one of them.

"So positive were they, and so overwhelmingly happy that the father couldn't stand their simple arguments, but was compelled to believe what they were telling him was true, and he also began to praise the Lord and to participate in their joy.

This is the house in which the angel appeared to the children in Dark county, Ohio. A friend of mine took the picture for this book.

"This simple story has been told to only a few of their most intimate friends. They deemed it too sacred to be told to everybody, lest they could not appreciate it. The writer became their pastor in the spring of 1896, and not until the evening of January 7, 1897, did they tell me about it; and the way it came about was this:

"Ida and Nettie had been to school during the day and the question came up whether, or not, the Lord revealed Himself to men now as He did in olden times through the ministry of angels. The teacher seemed to be skeptical, and said he did not believe such things were possible at the present time. He had never heard of this instance and therefore, knew nothing about it until Ida declared her belief in such things from the fact that they had seen an angel in their home when they were children. So when she came from school she was telling her mother what the teacher had said, and how she had convinced him contrary to his former belief. I overheard their conversation and began to wonder what they were talking about. Then they happened to think they had never told me the story and at once began to relate it. As the children were all at home they were soon seated around me and with shining faces were busily engaged in making known to me this remarkable incident, and it has made an

impression upon me that shall never leave me. While they were telling me I felt that such a good thing should not be kept secret any
longer. Therefore the day following I wrote out a minute account of
it, just as the children had told me. Of course, they were no longer
little children, for all, except Pearl, had grown up.

"The reader may imagine what a thrill of joy and gladness filled
my soul, while by the help of God I undertook to write this story.
Here I was in the very room where it occurred. To my left was the
same sofa upon which these children had their family worship on
the memorable night in February, ten years before. A little farther
on to the left was the very door through which the angel had come
and gone. To my right was the same rocking chair in which this
heavenly messenger had been seated. In my lap lay the same book,
opened at the very picture which had brought from them the wish
that they might see an angel once, and upstairs is the stove which he
said was nice.

"Nearly five years later (November 27, 1901), I visited them
again. All the children, except Ora, are still at home, and in the
evening while seated with them in the same room, and talking together about this same matter, I found that after the lapse of nearly
fifteen years it has not in the least lost its freshness in their memo-
ries. For with shining faces and with hearts glowing with gratitude
to God for His goodness to them, they still love to talk about the
wonderful visitor whom He, in His kind providence, had seen fit to
send them in the days of their childhood. Their whole lives have
been influenced by it."

Angels Visited My Friends

Here are extracts of letters from my friends. Since I do not know
whether or not they would want their names in print, I omit them. I
have their letters in my possession.

One friend wrote: "About twenty years ago five angels visited
me while I was at work on a linotype in New York City." 3

Another letter says: "I had been looking to God in prayer a great
deal, only doing what I had to for my family and home. I then had
three children about five, seven and nine years old. That evening I
had put them to bed early, and their father had gone with them, but I
sat up to prepare the clothes for an early wash the next morning.
That I had made no mistake in my Christian life (by being a Christian) was what my soul and mind was seeking to know. As I was

meditating God answered me right then by letting me see an angel standing by my side. When I first saw him I thought it was my husband coming out in his night clothes to get a drink of water from the sink beside me, so that took all the fright away from me. I then took a good look at him and knew him to be an angel. He withdrew, and I could see him no more."

Another friend writes: "On February 9, 1931, I saw a beautiful angel. He was standing by my bedside. He was about five and a half feet high. He appeared like a person about thirty years old, beautiful and erect as a soldier. His trousers were dark brown, somewhat like those worn by men on earth. His belt seemed to be pure gold, about four inches wide. He had on a white shirt with green pin stripes about one inch wide between which were fine green vines. The shirt was made with a yoke in front with box plait effect and stood out full. The shirt was tucked back under the belt. His face was bright and shining.

"This was about eleven o'clock at night. Suddenly there was a light above the brightness of the sun upon my window shade, and all my room became flooded with light. As I wondered what caused the light, I saw the form by my bed.

" 'What is it?' I said.

" 'An angel of the Lord', he replied.

" 'I will arise and look at the angel of the Lord', I said.

" 'I cast my eyes upon his beautiful form only a second, when he said, 'Like unto the Son of Man', and vanished."

In Bible times angels appeared as men and they some times thus appear today. A nurse who had been caring for a very ill patient for five weeks, wrote: "One evening a friend came in to set the table. Then a strong, stalwart angel appeared. When my friend and I went to our dear one (she could be left alone only a short time) the angel went with us. He said, 'I will restore her to health.' He stood upon the foot of the bed for a short time, then spreading out his beautiful wings, vanished through the wall. The woman recovered."

On another occasion, she says: "I was standing in the kitchen when I heard the rustling of a heavenly being coming down the back stairs. An angel appeared, clothed in beautiful, dazzling robes of glory that reached to his ankles. He stood about four feet from me. Immediately I began to tremble. Two or three times I heard the words, 'Fear not, Mary.' I tried to obey and steady myself. The angel then communed with me about all that had happened on the day when we fasted and prayed. Having finished the conversation, he vanished through the walls; but, oh, the manifestation of the power of God he left behind ! It filled the place. I cried out: 'O God, if your people could only feel this power the angel left, they would never doubt again.' "

Where the angels are the presence of God is, for angels are endued with the power of God.

Angels Strengthen in Soul-Travail

Angels came to strengthen Jesus when in soul-travail in Gethsemane. They still come to strengthen His people in times of distress. Pastor Chilling, much used of the Lord, when but a young Christian in Germany, was in terrible perplexity. The pastor, whom he loved and in whom he had every confidence, was found to be a deep-seated hypocrite living in awful sin. Chilling, shattered in faith, was in the greatest agony. Should he give up religion? What should he do ? When in soul-distress in his room an angel suddenly appeared, shining with such heavenly glory-light that the whole room was lighted. Smiling upon the perplexed young man the angel, raising one hand above his head, pointed up and then disappeared. The distressed man was strengthened. His faith returned, and he became a useful servant of the Lord.

Angels Walked and Talked With Sundar Singh

Many times the angels ministered to Sundar Singh on his lonesome and dangerous itineraries to Tibet. When he was tied to a tree and left alone in a wilderness an angel loosed his bonds and brought him food. Another time he was cast into a deep well to sink into the decaying mass of putrid human bodies, and the cover of the pit was closed and locked. From this nauseous pit, in whose poisonous odors any man would suffocate, an angel unlocked the door and lifted him out. Thus we are reminded of Daniel's angelic deliverance from the pit and of Peter's liberation from the locked jail. Once, tired and lonesome, as he walked alone, this "apostle of bleeding feet" was comforted and renewed in strength by an angel. On another occasion forty Tibetans, intending to kill him, chased him into a mountain cave, but there they saw white- dressed angels whose feet did not touch the ground. and in fear the Tibetans fled. Sundar Singh, glorified from Tibet, is now with the saints and angels in heaven where he had been caught up so often to talk with them. He can tell us the rest of his angel stories as we sit by the river in Paradise.

Where saints abide angels minister. Where saints go angels accompany them. To help them pray, to guide their thoughts in holy ways, to bring a sure sense of the presence of God, angels thus help saints on earth to move upward in the degrees of heaven. But this ministry, usually invisible, is hindered by the opposition of evil spirits as well as by the depraved natures of our own mortal bodies, which act as walls hindering our own direct fellowship with the angels.

But the angels are here. We live among them, and they hover over us. They help guide us through this vale of mortal tears until we complete this stage of the journey of life. There may be persecutions. This is the appointed lot of every child of God. There may be suffering and hardship; there may be stripes and prisons. This is the way the Savior trod; it is the way His own must travel. But to those who work in His will all is well. No more persecutions will come than is for our good or the good of the Kingdom of God, and no more stripes will be our lot than Jesus allows us to bear. When we suffer, we shall suffer in the will of God. And when we should be delivered, stocks, and swords, and guns, and locked doors cannot hold us, for "He shall give His angels charge over thee to keep thee in all thy ways. (Ps. 91:11).

ANGELS SERVING ON EARTH

With the angels here below,
We should surely learn to know
How to make the Lord our choice;
With the angels all about
As we move here in and out,
We should learn to hear their voice.

Guardian angels, with their power
Protecting, keep us, hour by hour,
Out of dangers, one by one;
And the angels vigils keep,
While in child-like peace we sleep
Till our work on earth is done.

Angels, with their tender care,
Now are here and everywhere

Bringing heaven's glory down;
While the devil's demons stare
At the blessing we can share,
Till we get our golden crown.

They may come to us unseen,
Or may come to us as men—
Or as lightning from the skies;
But, the angels in their love,
All the saints will lead above
As a resurrection prize.

CHAPTER 14
WHO ARE BEST PREPARED TO SERVE WITH THE ANGELS?

Suffering Saints Prepared To Be Serving Saints

Those who suffer for Christ upon earth and "enter the Kingdom of God through tribulation" (Acts 14:22) are exalted to highest service there. Willingly and deliberately enduring hardship for Christ they enter the highest plains in heaven. It is upon this earth where Jesus died that we prepare ourselves for service among the saints in heaven.

Talmage wrote of what he saw in heaven: "I appreciated for the first time what Paul said to Timothy, 'If we suffer we shall reign with Him.' It surprised me beyond description that all the great in heaven were great sufferers. Not all? Yes, all. There was Moses, David, Ezekiel, yea all the apostles, who after lives of suffering, died by violence: beaten to death with fuller's clubs or dragged to death by mobs, or from the thrust of sword, or by exposure on barren island, or by decapitation.

"All high up in heaven had been great sufferers, and women more than men. Felicitas, and St. Cecilia, and St. Agnes, and St. Agatha, and St. Lucia, and women never heard of outside their own neighborhood; queens of the needle, and the washtub, and the dairy, rewarded according to how well they did their work, whether to set a table or govern a nation, whether empress or milkmaid."

Another person, led up to heaven's higher plains, says she caught a glimpse of the place from which Jesus, almost two thousand years ago, went away to prepare for those who love Him. She saw the white light which glorified the faces of those who basked in its radiance, and she saw missionaries and others who had done slum work in the city. She says further:

"It seemed that those who had suffered most for Jesus' sake, those who 'had come up out of great tribulation' were the ones whose faces shone with the most glorious light."

The greater the suffering for Jesus, the greater the exaltation in heaven. The heavier the cross born on earth, the higher the plain reached in heaven. The higher the plain, the more radiant the glory light in which the saint will live, and the more his face will be Christ-like and his glorified body emanate the light in which he lives and serves. The more we suffer for Christ now, the better we can serve Him in heaven.

General Booth was allowed to see some of the marshaled hosts of heaven, and he says:

"What a sight that was! Worth toiling a lifetime to be hold it! Nearest the King were the patriarchs and apostles of ancient times. Next, rank after rank, came the holy martyrs who had died for Him. Then came the army of warriors who had fought for Him in every part of the world; and around and about, above and below, I beheld myriads of spirits who were never heard of outside their own neighborhoods, or beyond their own times, who with self-denying zeal and untiring toil had labored to extend God's kingdom and to save souls of men.

"Encircling this gorgeous scene above, beneath, around, hovered glittering angelic beings who had kept their first estate, proud, it seemed to me, to minister to the happiness and exaltation of those redeemed out of the poor world whence I came.

"I was bewildered by the scene. The songs, the music, the shouts of the multitude came like the roar of a thousand cataracts, echoed and re-echoed through the glory-lit mountains, and the magnificent and endless army of happy spirits ravished my senses with passionate delight."

Then the King addressed General Booth who, until that time, had lived a nominal, useless, lazy, professing Christian life, and said:

"Thou wilt feel thyself little in harmony with these, once the companions of my tribulation and now of my glory, who counted not their lives dear unto themselves in order to bring honor to me and salvation to men." And he gave a look of admiration at the host of apostles and martyrs and warriors gathered around Him.

"Oh, that look of Jesus! I felt that to have one such loving recognition would be worth dying a hundred deaths at the stake, worth being torn asunder by wild beasts. The angelic escort felt it, too, for their responsive burst of praise shook the very skies and the ground on which I lay.

"Then the King turned His eyes on me again. How I wished that some mountain would fall upon me and hide me forever from His presence! But I wished in vain. Some invisible and irresistible force compelled me to look up, and my eyes met His once more. I felt, rather than heard, Him saying to me in words that engraved themselves as fire upon my brain: 'Go back to earth, I will give you another opportunity. Prove thyself worthy of my name. Show to the world that thou possess my Spirit by doing My work and becoming, on My behalf, a savior of men.'

"'Thou shalt return hither (to heaven) when thou hast finished the battle, and I will give thee a place in my conquering train and a share in my glory!"

The harder the journey and the greater the suffering in service for Jesus now, the better the preparation to appreciate the glories of heaven and to serve Him there who gave His all for us.

Heaven and the Angels

When the Lord led General Booth and others to heaven to see the glory and exalted state of those who suffer most for Jesus and endure most for Him in saving men, it was not for the good of those heavenly visitors only, but for us as well. The Lord wants it made known to all His people that the highest privilege of man is to humble himself low and suffer much for Jesus' sake and man's salvation.

An Advantage To Be Saved On Earth

It is a great advantage to be saved on earth. Here alone is the opportunity to overcome foes while in the flesh; here alone is the possibility of suffering for Jesus; here alone is the chance to endure the contradictions of sinners; in this life alone can the saint be persecuted by evil men, be reviled and answer not again, be hated and hate not, be slain as a lamb before the shearers is dumb and answereth not a word. Here is the only place to die for Jesus' sake and for the sake of the Gospel of Christ. The one chance to give all to Jesus is this present body of flesh on this earth. Those who see this truth and embrace it, and rejoice in it, and regulate their actions by it, will one day be blessed by calls to higher service on higher plains of glory in Gloryland. "They who suffer with Him will reign with Him."

John saw the company of saints who live on the highest plain in highest heaven, those who stand on Mount Zion and are at home about the Throne of God and the Lamb. These are they who follow the Lamb whithersoever He goeth: into degradation, rejection, humiliation and persecution by scribes and Pharisees to be spit upon, to be scourged, to be bound and to be crucified amidst scoffs and jeers. Those who follow the Lamb through suffering on earth are the Lord's most beloved, and follow Him whithersoever He goeth in heaven. Who, in Paradise, can live as near to Jesus as those who died on this fallen earth in giving their lives for many? Angels would covet the privilege of being saved on earth that they might save earth's men from destruction.

It is a great advantage to be saved early and live long for the Lord on earth. Here is the only place we have a chance to suffer and die as Jesus did for the salvation of men. One of these men said he sometimes hoped Jesus would not come just yet, for he wanted to endure more and work more for Him before He came.

There is a song that angels in heaven cannot sing, a song that none of the saints in the lower plains of glory can sing. There is a song whose distilled sweetness none can sing, save those who suffer most for Jesus. "And I heard a voice from heaven, as the voice of many waters, and as the voice of great thunder: and I heard the voice of harpers harping with their harps; and they sang, as it were, a new song before the four beasts and the elders: and no man could learn that song, but the hundred and forty and four thousand which were redeemed from the earth—and in their mouth was found no guile, for they are without fault before the throne of God." (Rev. 14:5). This is the song that martyrs and great sufferers can sing.

A Right and A Wrong Teaching

A widespread teaching in a different strain appears, and it carries a different undertone. It seems to sing in soul-pleasing strains that, in the days of stress coming upon the earth, the predominating purpose of the Church of the Lord is to escape tribulation, flee from the sting of the lash and get away from the anguish of the cross. Can it be that those who are counted worthy to stand before the throne of God and in the presence of the Lamb that was slain have found some other way to appear to sing the "new song" no others can sing? Is there another way than through tribulation to be able to sing the new song? Can it be that Jesus will smile His loving approval upon some others unless it be for those who have suffered more for Him on earth? They who willingly, deliberately and purposefully bared their backs to the iron-pointed lash and spared not the flesh from the agony of torturous death—these are the favored of the Crucified, the Bible and the cloud of witnesses affirm.

Suffering is the message of the Old Testament; it is the message the resurrected Christ gave the Apostle John to "write to all the churches"; and it is the message Jesus has given some of His chosen and most used servants on earth to carry back to mortal man after their revelation of heaven. That the greatest sufferers for Christ's sake are the most honored in heaven is the message made known to men from the days of Adam down through each century. Those who steadfastly set their faces toward their earthly Jerusalem with the afflictions and the cross there awaiting them, will be those who stand before the throne of God worthy to sing the song of Moses and the Lamb. They "came out of great tribulation." Therefore are they before the throne of God and serve Him day and night in His temple; and He that sitteth on the throne shall dwell among them— the Lamb, which is in the midst of the throne, shall feed them, and shall lead them into living fountains of waters." (Rev. 7:14-17).

"I was bewildered by the scene. The songs, the music, the shouts of the multitude came like a roar of a thousand cataracts [waterfalls], echoed and re-echoed through the glory-lit mountains." This was the exultation and praise and songs in heaven of those who counted not their lives dear unto themselves in order to bring honor to Christ and salvation to men.

Bunyan, General Booth, and many others had been living easy lives on earth, escaping tribulation, when caught up to the city of God to see its order. Their eyes being opened to the truth of heavenly values, they plead for one more chance to relive their lives, so that they might better serve Christ by suffering and enter heaven's glories through tribulation on earth. Let us make no mistake, seeing we are compassed about by such "a great cloud of witnesses." Should we not seek to suffer as He suffered, rather than covet a place on His right hand, or on His left, that by our suffering and conforming unto His death, we might by all means save some? Not for our own glory, not for high seats in heaven, but that others may be saved, we are glad to suffer the loss of all things and count not our lives dear unto ourselves.

In view of the eternal values of serving and suffering on this earth, should not the understanding Christian desire, for Jesus' sake and glory, to live as long as possible on the earth? To save more souls and get better training for higher service should be our aim. No wonder the angels in heaven told one visitor that it should be the desire of every Christian to live as long as possible.

Service through hardships on earth must be an unselfish service. It must be a service of love for Jesus, love for sinners and love for other Christians. "Though I bestow all my goods to feed the poor, and though I give my body to be burned, and have not love it profiteth nothing." (1 Cor. 13:3).

Every saint and angel in heaven sees through our motives. All, including ourselves, will see the motives of our hearts, the real reason for our sufferings and sacrifices.

When the motives are right—living unreservedly for Jesus and the salvation of men—we shall be prepared for more important service, either on earth or in heaven, in the building up the saints, whether in this present age, or in the next age of one thousand years, or in other ages to come.

Greatness in heaven is in proportion to loving service. Jesus expects us to learn the secrets of this high service by suffering and giving upon this earth. To serve Him faithfully in all His house, to do His bidding in small or large things, to accomplish His assignments through any tribulation, even unto death, and then at the end have Him look at us personally with the smile that lights all heaven and say: "Well done, good and faithful servant!" will be reward enough to repay any saint for entering the kingdom of God through great tribulation.

Jesus dying on the cross is at times manifested to the inhabitants of heaven — saints and angels. Those who most sacrificially go to heaven, the cross-way, by bearing the cross here, will reach the realms the nearest the Crucified One.

SAINTS BEST PREPARED TO SERVE IN HEAVEN

The saints who are saved by the blood of the Lamb,
To dwell in the realms of the One Great I Am:
Will each, in the order of the things up above,
In the heavenly plains, in the land of His love

Be assigned the work in the land that is New,
In accord with the work they are able to do.
What we do when we're here, assigns work for us there,
For we do only that for which now we prepare.

If we live at our ease, to enjoy only bliss
And the way of the cross, in this way, we should miss,
In heaven, in shame, we then surely will stand
As we gaze on the feet and the nail-pierced hand.

It's the way of the cross, and the thorns in the face
That saved us poor sinners, by love and by grace,
To suffer and die, as did Christ in our stead,
That others, like us, may be raised from the dead.

The cross that avails over devils and death
Is the cross we should bear as long as we've breath.
The cross is the way; the cross is our lot;
To help bear the cross by the blood, we are bought.

If the cross, for our Savior, we daily shall bear,
For service in heaven we better prepare;
The martyrs stand nearest to Christ in His love,
For this is the order in heaven above.

To bear crosses on earth is a wonderful gain
To all who forever in heaven would reign.
Now is the time we should count all a loss,
And the time to help save by our own bloody cross.

CHAPTER 15
The Way to Heaven With the Angels

To see clearly the highway that leads to heaven where the angels are and to be certain that we are on that road are the things of supreme importance—eternal importance. Having found this way of life, it should then be the consuming purpose of every redeemed person so to walk and work in the will of God as to make his usefulness of greatest value to the Lord. This consuming purpose will also pre pare him for greatest capacity to appreciate life in heaven with the angels and fit him for highest service there.

To be unquestionably on the right path is the thing of supreme importance. "I am the Way, the Truth and the Life: No man cometh unto the Father, but by Me." (John 14:6). "He that hath the Son hath life (eternal life, hath the Holy Spirit). He that hath not the Son (by the indwelling Holy Spirit) hath not life." (1 John 4:12).

Who Are the Saved?

The way to heaven is clear. Those who have committed their past sins and their future lives entirely to Jesus are saved and on their way to heaven. Their real purpose is to repent, that is, to forsake sin and do the will of Christ. They believe that Jesus, "His own self, bare our sins in His own body on the tree"—died in the sinner's place. (1 Peter 2:24).

In other words, Jesus takes the sinner's place on the cross, while the sinner is reckoned as having all the perfection of Jesus' righteousness. In Jesus the sinner becomes righteous, holy and sinless. This righteousness, reckoned to the repentant sinner, now a saint, is independent of his works or the amount of sin committed in the past. It is a gift. "The gift of God is eternal life." Salvation is an unmerited, unearned favor given "by grace", not "by works", or by moral character and virtue in man. (Eph. 2:8,9).

The redeemed are saved by faith, "He that believeth hath eternal life." (John 5:24). He believes that Jesus is the Son of God—is God come in the flesh. He believes that Jesus bears his sin and accepts him, a sinner, but now a son. He believes the Scripture, which says that Jesus was "made to be sin" (considered a sinner) for us, who knew no sin, that we might be made the righteousness of God (be as righteous as God) in Him. (2 Cor. 5:21). "He died for all that they which live (the saved) should not henceforth live unto themselves (be selfish), but unto Him which died for them and rose again." (2 Cor. 5:15).

He whose sins are washed in Jesus' blood becomes as sinless as a child who never sinned. All his sins are gone and forgotten. The sure Word of God says it. Believe it.

Life in Jesus

Jesus gives His Holy Spirit to all who become His sons. The sinner, now become a saint, receives as a down payment a measure of the Holy Spirit which energizes him to act as a heavenly citizen. He is inspired to serve his Savior. By the Holy Spirit he is thus born again, "born from above", made a "new creature in Christ." Henceforth he has an inflow from above and a constant indwelling of the Holy Spirit, the life of Christ. "If any man be in Christ he is a new creature." 1(2 Cor. 5:17).

In other words, if a man does not have a change of heart and a new life he is not a "new creature", is not in Christ, is not saved. He will not get into the New Jerusalem with the saints and angels.

When, by grace, God saves a man, He does a double work. On the one hand He takes away the man's sins. He cleanses the sinner. The cleansing in Jesus' blood from all past sins is complete. Not a past sin will the Lord ever bring up again on earth, or in heaven, to humiliate and condemn him. "Their sins and iniquities will I remember no more." (Heb. 10:17).

Moreover, the Lord, having completely cleaned up the past life of the sinner by His grace, He causes him to live differently from other people. God's guarantee reads: "This is the covenant—I will put my laws into their mind (new purposes) and write them in their hearts." (Heb. 8:10). A new life from God. A gift. Eternal life. Heaven begun now.

They who will spend eternity in Paradise above must now, in this present earth, drink of the waters of life that flow from heaven. "Whosoever drinketh of the water that I shall give him shall never thirst (perish); but the water that I shall give him shall be in him a

well of water (the Holy Spirit) springing up into everlasting life."
John 4:14; 7:37-39.

Faith Brings Works

Although salvation is "by faith apart from works", the faith that
saves a sinner is not a dead faith, or a passive faith. Saving faith is
active faith, a faith that comes from God, not only enabling him
with new purposes and energy "to do" the work of God. Thus, saving faith is also working faith. "Faith, if it hath not works, is
dead." (James 2:17).

A man does not work to "get saved." He works to please Christ
because he is saved. He works not to win Christ. He works because
Christ won him. He serves Jesus because Jesus first served him and
gave Himself for him. "His sheep hear His voice and follow Him."
They owe their all to Him who died for them. With Him, and in
Him, they also died, were buried, and rose again to be like Him.
They give their lives for the world to complete the work of their
Savior in saving men. As Jesus came to seek and save the lost, so do
His sons go out to seek and save lost men.

The nearer the redeemed sons of God approach the unselfish
likeness and perfection of Christ in their character and in their service on earth, the nearer will they live to Him in heavenly mansions
in the land of the glorified.

If We Sin

If the redeemed man sins, he is sorry. If he falls into disgrace he
is ashamed, not so much because of the loss of his own reputation,
but because he has brought reproach on the name of Jesus, His Redeemer. Because of appreciation for what Jesus did for him on the
cross and for what Jesus does for him through the Holy Spirit, the
truly saved person will not, and cannot, live in persistent sin. "Sin
shall not have dominion over you." (Rom. 6:14).

Jesus Keeps Him

The converted person does not hold Jesus; Jesus holds him. Although he does make mistakes and sometimes sins, the Holy Spirit
within him convicts him of his sin, speaks to his conscience and
persuades him to repent and confess his sins to God, and be
cleansed afresh in Jesus' blood.

If he is stubborn Jesus chastises him, "for whom the Lord loveth he chastises, and scourgeth every son whom he receiveth." (Heb. 12:6). The Lord does not disown His stubborn child, or disinherit him. He whips him hard with lash-cutting stripes until he becomes obedient.

An Overcomer An Outcomer

How can we emphasize enough that the overcomer is an outcomer? "What fellowship hath righteousness with unrighteousness, and what communion hath light with darkness, or what part hath a believer with an infidel?—I will dwell in them and walk in them: and I will be their God, and they shall be my people." "Wherefore, come out from among them, and be ye separate, saith the Lord, and touch not the unclean thing; and I will redeem you. And I will be a father unto you, and ye shall be my sons and daughters, saith the Lord Almighty." (2 Cor. 6:14-18).

Those on the highway to gloryland are they who, having turned their backs on the things behind — the works of the world, the flesh and the devil — now whole-heartedly have made Jesus and the things above their one great choice.

Again we say that he who will dwell with the angels and Jesus in heaven is the one who prefers such fellowship while still dwelling down here on earth. He will so love heavenly fellowship that he will gladly now forsake the sins and ambitions of the present world. He will be "different." He will not be "one of them." He has "come out" of the world. He belongs to the new and high heavenly order. He "practices" the life of heaven so much among earthly men that they see and know he belongs to a different sphere.

Life in Jesus Alone

There is no way to heaven but the Jesus way—the unselfish way, the dead-to-self way, the resurrection way. Not doctrine, not interpretations of Scripture, nor anything else, except new life direct from Jesus will save us and make us fellow-servants with the saints and angels in heaven.

Profession Not Possession

From the foregoing it is apparent that the majority of professing Christians are not really Christians at all. They do not follow Christ, do not serve Him any sacrifice, and are not truly in love with Him. They are not infatuated with Jesus. They are not His.

On the other hand, in almost every church a little group of real "lovers" do love Jesus most of all. They serve Him the best they can with what light they have. They are saved and they know it and they act like it. They love Christ rather than the things of the world. They love to advance the kingdom of God more than to do anything else. They seriously live for Jesus' sake and His glory—not for self. They are members of His little flock on earth who will one day join the great united multitude to sing before the throne of God the praises of their Redeemer.

Salvation a Reality

We are dealing with realities. Salvation is something real, at experience. Who wants theory? We want fact. Who wants to suppose he is saved, to hope he is saved, to be trying to be saved? We want the fact, the experience of salvation. Since salvation is something to get, we want to "get it" and get it so unmistakably that we cannot doubt that we have it, despite all the disconcerting efforts of devils and hell. Knowing the tremendous eternal issues at stake, is it not worth the effort to "make our calling and election sure?" It can be done. It must be done.

The saved man, the real citizen of heaven does not live in uncertainty while still on earth. We once were spiritually dead. Now we are alive—a great difference, and we know it "We know we have passed out of death unto life, because we love the brethren (Christians)." (1 John 3:14). "Hereby know we that we dwell in Him and He in us, because He hath given us of His spirit." (1 John 4:13).

Through the Holy Spirit the crucifixion of Christ in our stead for our sins can become more real than were we with human eyes to see this take place. Our sins washed away in Jesus' blood can be as real in our experience as is bathing our body in water. The removal of the burden of our sins can be in actual experience as definite a transaction as if a friend lifted from our bodies a hundred-pound weight that held us down. The Holy Spirit can come into our hearts as definitely as a man enters the door of a house. "Know ye not that your bodies are the temples of the Holy Spirit"? (1 Cor. 6:19). The Holy Spirit can come into the heart of a saved man, giving him as definite a birth from above as that of a child born into the physical world. The child cries, but knows not that it cries. The child of God, born by the Holy Spirit into the spiritual world, also cries. He cries, "Abba, Father", from the Spirit-endued inner being, and he knows that he cries. He knows that he is born. "The Spirit itself beareth witness with our spirit that we are the children of God." (Rom. 8:16). "He that believeth on the Son of God hath the witness in himself. (1 John 5:10).

Without any visions like those related in this volume, without hearing any audible voices from heaven (which some unmistakably hear) it is possible under the anointing of the Holy Spirit to experience and know more of the realities of heaven and the angels than I have been able to put into words in all this book. I testify from experience that all I write about the reality, the fact of salvation and the work of the Holy Spirit is true. Multitudes of God's people in every land under the sun can also verify this from their experiences. Here we deal with facts, not theories. We are talking about facts as sure as any facts in the universe. The facts about salvation through Christ are facts that you, or I, or anyone, can test and find true by experience. If you doubt this, try it. Anyone who comes to Christ in the Bible-way will experience the facts of salvation the Bible says he will experience. Have you tried it in the Bible way? If not, try it. You will not be disappointed. You will never have a regret. You will get a true experience for which you will praise God throughout eternity.

In view of this, surely no one will be satisfied to stop short of entering into the life that will make him one with the realities of heaven and the angels.

Seek the Treasure

If any man will spend the time and effort seeking God that men on earth spend seeking perishable treasures, he will certainly find unsearchable riches. If any man, by honest prayer and fasting, will seek heavenly food for his soul as diligently as he seeks daily bread for his body, "he will surely find hidden manna", the real "bread of life"—Jesus. Since heaven and the angels are all about us, it is possible to pray through the clouds and get salvation any where—on a mountain side, walking along the road, at home, or in a crowd. But, like the saints in heaven from higher plains, help those on lower plains, and like the stronger saints on all plains, help the weaker, serving in love, so it is here on earth. The stronger and older saints can help the younger and weaker. A man is most likely to get saved when among saints who know God themselves and have Christ in them. Such saints can best help the sinner to find the Lamb of God who taketh away the sins of the world. Likewise a person may get the baptism of the Holy Spirit anywhere, but he is most likely to get it among those who already have the baptism. From their higher plain, by serving in love those who have the baptism of the Holy Spirit they can help those on lower plains of spiritual experience up into these higher realms of glory.

No sect, or church, or denomination is altogether perfect. When all the truth contained in all the churches is combined it must be admitted that, at best, heaven's truth is seen "through a glass darkly" when compared with all the wonders and unfathomed mysteries of heaven. This being true, we should be humble and help one another, those on higher plains serving in love those on lower plains. Those on lower plains, in turn, should be teachable as little children and be glad to receive truth from others without envy, jealousy, or strife. But it is not so.

Each saved person should certainly serve God where he can get the most love and life from heaven, where he can get the most strength from other saints, where he can get the most liberty in the Holy Spirit, and where his efforts for Christ will be the most efficient in saving men and building up the kingdom of God. Sect, or church, or place should be a very secondary consideration. Jesus' salvation, power in the Holy Spirit, service for Christ, the saving of sinners, the building up the body of Christ, should be put first, always first, everlastingly first. Loyalty to Christ and love to do all His will should far exceed any selfish or natural loyalty to kindred, or sect, or priest, or preacher. Not a thing or a person in all the world should be allowed to have preference over our purpose to receive all of heaven that Jesus means us to have. Nothing should be allowed to hinder us from doing all the work Jesus expects us to do in the power of the Holy Spirit. Jesus first, always first. No man on earth or in heaven will ever regret having put Jesus first. "Seek ye first the kingdom of God." (Matt. 6:33).

Jesus First and Last

Now we close this volume as we began—with Jesus. In exhausting a limited vocabulary in attempting to outline the glories of heaven, the aim has been to exalt Jesus above all. He is over all, in all and fills all heaven with Himself. Without Him there is no heaven; with Him it is heaven everywhere.

Today is the day to start all over again and give our sins, our failures, our life, and our all to Jesus in absolute abandon. To do this is to find heaven here in the shadows and the angels about us. It is to find Jesus and eternal life.

And now, from heaven, Jesus comes again! Is He not walking by the shore where we perform our daily tasks and gently saying, "Leave your nets and follow me and I will make you fishers of men?" Those who come to him He will in no wise cast out. He will mold and make them again "into the image of God."

It is all a question of life in Jesus who says, "Behold, I stand at the door and knock: if any man hear my voice and open the door I will come in to him, and will sup with him, and he with me. To him that overcometh will I grant to sit with me on my throne" (Rev. 3:20,21). What an offer! What an astonishing proposition! Who would not accept it?

Jesus' love for wayward men is written in letters of gold all through the Bible. On its last page in a heart-yearning exhortation Jesus holds out His loving nail-pierced hands with these words: "Let him that heareth come, let him that is athirst come. Whosoever will, let him take the water of life freely. (Rev. 22:17).

Come to Him. He takes away the sins which separate us from heaven. Come to Him. His angels descend about us. Come to Him and become eternal heirs to jeweled mansions by the golden streets in the paradise of the glorified. Come to Him, and Jesus becomes our life, in us, and we, in Him, now and throughout the numberless ages.

"Verily I say unto you—He that believeth on him—hath everlasting life, and will not come into condemnation." (John 5:24). He who comes is made clean from every sin and sin- stain; he is clothed in spotless robes of white; he is washed in Jesus' blood and clothed with His righteousness. He is made ready for life on earth, or life in heaven.

Their sins and their iniquities will I remember no more. (Heb. 10:17). Sins forgiven. Sins gone. Sins remembered no more— forgotten !

Lord, I come. Just as I am without one plea, save that my Savior Jesus died for me.

I accept Jesus as my Savior. I believe that He died on the cross for me. I believe that His blood cleanses me from all sin. Henceforth I will, by His grace and enabling power, live only for Him, who gave His life for me, and gladly will I serve Him by life or death

Sign here:

....

Make this surrender and acceptance in audible words.

Act your faith by immediate obedience to the will of God in water baptism. Be buried in water, completely buried, as evidence that you believe you have been buried with Christ—the old man buried with all his sins, and risen in life to live forever in His resurrection life.

"He that believeth and is baptized shall be saved." "Repent and be baptized every one of you in the name of Jesus Christ for the remission of sins, and ye shall receive the gift of the Holy Ghost." "And now, why tarriest thou? Arise, and be baptized, and wash away thy sins, calling on the name of the Lord." "Know ye not that so many of us as were baptized into Jesus Christ were baptized into His death?" "Therefore, we are buried with Him by baptism into death: that like as Christ was raised up from the dead by the glory of the Father, even so we also should walk in newness of life. (Mark 16:16 Acts 2:38; Acts 22 :16; Rom. 6:3, 4).

THE WAY

The way that leads to the royal
Hill In the Paradise of God,
Is clear to the man who seeks
His will And the road that Jesus trod.

The way is bright as day after night,

To the man who turns his back
On the things of self and things not right,
To follow a cross-bearing track.

The way is one that a fool can find,
If he wants a change of heart
And is willing to leave the world behind
To make a different start.

The way of life is the way of death,
By nail-pierced feet and hands:
It starts at the cross, at the final breath
Of Him from Glory-lands.
The way that leads to the land so fair,
To the land of pure delight:
Is made for the man who is well aware
Of his sinful, self-willed plight.

This way he will find at the foot of the cross,
If he kneels down there to pray
And reckons his sins and his life a loss,
And gives His all away.

The way he will find is free from sin,
For Jesus died in his stead;
Who now forgives and cleanses him,
And gives him His Spirit which raises the dead.

****

The Scripture appendix that was in the original edition of this book has been removed because the Scripture references were put inside the book, rather than having the reader look them up here at the end of the book.

Made in United States
North Haven, CT
30 May 2023

37172927R00095